The Smartphone Addiction Restriction

It's Almost Too Late…

A CONCERNED CITIZEN

PUBLISHING

advice. The content within this book has been derived from various sources. Please consult a licensed professional before attempting any techniques outlined in this book.

By reading this document, the reader agrees that under no circumstances is the author responsible for any losses, direct or indirect, that are incurred as a result of the use of the information contained within this document, including, but not limited to, errors, omissions, or inaccuracies.

Table of Contents

Introduction

Have you seen the 1999 action sci-fi film *The Matrix*? It is a mind-bending movie, especially for its time. I rewatched it recently and came to three conclusions: Keanu Reeves has aged about 10 years since 1999 (the vampire rumors are right!); CGI has gotten better (I never imagined CGI could get better at the time of first watching it, the CGI seemed flawless back then); and that the movie was incorrectly categorized… There was action galore, for sure!

It's the 'fiction' part of the label of 'science fiction' that stood out to me; I look around today and see that society is plugged into computers. They're in almost every room of our homes - cell phones, gaming consoles, tablets, laptops and PCs nearly everywhere you look. Nowadays, *The Matrix* is closer to a 'dramatization' than 'fiction.' Hollywood created a cool-looking 'fiction,' but real-life is an awful horror. This is a problem and you know it - isn't that why you are reading this book? Something is wrong and we need to wake up to it.

Our society is broken in such a way that this run-away train is not going to stop until we're derailed. If you were to pick up your phone, how many apps could you say you have? Are there ones that you don't recognize, some that you downloaded and never opened? It's likely that there are and it's no coincidence, if you compare the global turnover of physical goods versus the digital market, you may be shocked to find out exactly what the average Joe spends his money on. The reason I bring this up is to say: breweries love alcoholics; tobacco manufacturers love addicts; do you think big-tech is any different?

Who are the ultra-rich guys right now? Bezos, Gates, and those like them. For household names like Amazon; Apple; Facebook; Google; Microsoft - what do successful companies do? "Research and Development," right? You can see you are the lab rat, we all are. Let me just say that I'm a proponent of progress, I love what I can do with my Smartphone! What I don't like is what Smartphones can do with me if I give in to the temptation.

Having a beer while watching the Sunday game is great, but if you're struggling to stay sober - daily - you have a problem. The sad thing is that being 'tech-drunk' is okay in society. There are daily occurrences of road accidents caused by texting-while-driving syndrome! Yes, it really is a syndrome. You'd have to be insane to think that operating a heavy vehicle at 60 miles/hour blindfolded is a good idea. I say blindfolded because when you're texting and driving, you aren't seeing anything but that screen.

The obvious temptation to "migrate your life to the cloud" is fueled by more than coincidence. As I previously mentioned, there's big money in the digital revolution. There is a corporate ethical issue that no one is addressing on any significant scale. Should tobacco or alcohol companies be allowed to advertise on television? Similarly, should gaming app developers be allowed to hire psychologists and actuarial scientists to tap into your addictive behavior complex? Do you think it is a coincidence that so many gaming apps (of a common genre) share basic principles? Don't even get me started on the 30-day login bonuses that reset to 'day 1' if you give it a break for a day.

There are very few industries that have been able to utilize all the dirty tricks of marketing and 'mind hacks' without limitations. But get an actuary to work out how many timers working on however many tiers of value a developer needs to code to make sure you are stuck with the following dilemma: "Its 10 PM now, I need to get up for work [or school] at 6 AM, so if I play till 2 AM I should be good, yeah?" The cellphone gaming industry is worth billions per year - possibly more than $100,000,000,000 by 2023, by some predictions. That is a lot of zeros to keep them interested in how they can get your buy-in. Either you are paying or an advertiser is - either way, the industry makes money by keeping you on your phone for as long as possible.

It is amazing to see a 70-year-old granny sitting on the bus playing *SomethingCrush* on her phone. *The Matrix*: we are a plugged-in society. (It is impressive that so many grannies can use a touch-screen though.)

Don't get me wrong, it is undoubtedly a good thing that you can run a business out of your phone or laptop. I remember a time, back when the world was in black-and-white, when a phonebook was a book, and if you wanted to look up something you had to go to a library. I love that it's now as easy as saying: "Siri…" Progress is something we should be proud of, like discovering how to use fire. And, like fire, technology makes a wonderful servant but a horrible master. Who is in charge? Your phone is dying and you are hungry, where do you go - to get your charger or to the refrigerator? You go to the outlet because it is quicker, right? So how long does your stomach have to wait while you are tethered to the wall? For a lot of people, Maslow's "hierarchy of needs" should really be rearranged where our phone/laptop/TV comes before sleeping or eating.

That is exactly why you are reading this, because you agree. Society is broken, right? Things are far from hopeless though. There is a simple solution: kick the smartphone addiction. Tech-junkies are like heroin-junkies. I am dead serious; it's a brain-chemistry thing. Tech addiction is a *bona fide* addiction and even has an "Anonymous" group like AA. We will get into that later. All you have to do is develop the unplugging habit and you'll be able to enjoy the conveniences of technology, guilt-free. Plus, as a bonus, you can experience life as something greater than just someone else's cash-cow.

So if this is you, or if you are reading this for the sake of a loved one (parents, I am here for you too), we are going to run through a bit of theory; a few fun facts; one-too-many pop-culture references; and *everything you need to become a human again*. The sad part is that I wish this was way more complex (I *so* want to seem as smart as one of those actuaries), but it's actually super simple and easy. The hardest part is just not being glued to your Twitter feed 24-7.

Chapter 1:

Addiction

It is important to understand how addiction works to overcome it. Our mind and body are very closely connected; our internal chemistry causes us to tend toward certain behavioral patterns and, in turn, our actions cause our body chemistry to change. Our actions affect our thoughts that then fuel our future actions. This is the mental aspect of addiction, addictions reinforce addictions.

Another aspect to consider is the physical part of addiction. The body adapts to new chemicals and then becomes dependent on them. Your body learns to 'need' what you give it again and again. When you stop giving it what it has become addicted to it goes into 'withdrawal.' Withdrawal can make you feel like you are dying, your thoughts become so obsessed with not having your 'fix' that rationality completely dissolves.

Think about the cranky smoker that hasn't had a cigarette all day. While cigarettes are not the most immediately harmful recreational drug on the market, they're still addictive, and consuming them regularly is detrimental. The cigarettes will still kill you in the long run, but, at least in the beginning, it is a relatively easy addiction to kick. It is easy to choose not to have cigarette #2 when one first tries a drag. Something like heroin is a different story, it is extremely physically addictive from the first hit. Addiction often kicks in on the first try.

But you already know not to do drugs (and also to stay in school), so why am I mentioning this? This is a book about electronic addiction, right? No one is putting anything dangerous or chemically addictive into their bodies, so what's with the biology lesson? Well, here is where this gets a bit complicated.

Heroin belongs to the opiate group. The reason opiates are so addictive is that they act in the same way as the naturally produced chemicals in our brains that are linked to our emotions. When you are raging, that blood-boiling feeling isn't just in your head, your body releases a hormone that enters your bloodstream and goes all over your body. This is also why it takes some time to cool down afterward - the naturally secreted chemical is still in your blood.

Ever know a guy that seems addicted to being angry? No matter what happens they 'need' to have a reason to be upset? And those optimists, no matter how dark the skies, must find a silver lining. How we interpret the events in our life gives our brain the context to decide what chemicals need to be pumped into our bloodstream. As mentioned, the only major difference between our neuro-chemistry and heroin is that a heroin-junky has no way of internally producing their drug - the chemicals affect our cells using the same mechanics.

We are all addicts in that way, it is human nature and biology. What we are aiming for is to be addicted to the chemicals that help our bodies (chemicals that support strong organ function), while avoiding the behaviors and substances that hurt our health - both physical and mental. We want to feel good and we also want to feel good about ourselves for acting the way we do.

How does this all tie into you spending 6 hours a day on your PS4? The answer is dopamine. We use different chemicals to tell our bodies how we feel and to get every cell to sync on what to feel. Dopamine is our 'satisfaction' chemical. We release it when we feel achievement or when we go into relaxation mode. Watching TV, playing a video game, checking social media feeds, and watching funny cat videos all stimulate dopamine release. Not to mention the design elements of shows and games that intentionally trigger 'achievement' responses. There are some very informative clips you can find on YouTube if you are a chemistry or biology follower.

It's not that bad, right? All these things are designed to make us feel good - no harm done to anyone - so what is the issue? There wouldn't be any issue if not for one factor: resistance. Just like the use of sugar - at first, we are very sensitive to a sugar spike. Think of kids on candy - they go ballistic. Add more sugar and we become desensitized or dependent. A little too much sugar and diabetes kicks in. Dopamine is the same: as a baby just standing for the first time brings total euphoria, even if only just for a second or two; it takes a much higher level of achievement to get a 7-year-old as excited and happy, and by the time they hit teen years, the 'emo' phase is a real concern for most parents.

Think of dopamine as sugar for a moment - how long will it take to develop diabetes? Wake up, check your phone - what's the weather? What's the latest on Twitter? Time to brush teeth - perfect Insta-moment! Who doesn't want to see you cleaning your teeth? Bowl of your favorite cereal goes down well with reading the news...paper? No, CNN has a website! Getting into the car for school or work - Bluetooth your Spotify playlist... We have barely begun the day and we have been tech-tethered all morning. If this was a spoon or two of sugar each time you touched your phone or turned on a screen, do you think you might be in the hospital by lunchtime?

The more dopamine we get, the less effective each dose becomes because of an ever-rising resistance. Too much sugar leads to insulin resistance. Our 'requirement' doesn't decrease though - like any drug user we need more and more of the substance to get the same 'fix.' The dopamine dose that was supplied in one hour of screen-time before now takes three hours of screen-time to get. Then six hours. Do you know of people that seem to be unable to go a solid hour without using some kind of electronic? This is an addiction, just like any other addiction you can think of.

And, just like any addiction, addicts find 'legitimate' excuses to support their addiction. The problem is that the overuse of technology is not easily associated with addiction, in the traditional sense. I think one reason why this is true is because a whole lot of us would have our sober self-image blown to bits if technology addiction was seen as an addiction. 'Addiction' is something often associated with criminals and social degenerates. Can good people suffer from addiction too? The answer is: "yes!"; as we mentioned, our bodies are addiction-inclined.

Addiction creates problems because it causes us to misalign our priorities. Crack cocaine addicts may go without eating to save money for their crack fixes. Hollywood has certainly shown us the lengths that addicts could go to get their fix - even children's cartoons show things like a mouse going to extraordinary lengths, even risking his life, to get his cheese fix. How many people can you think of that will avoid sleep to get in a few extra hours of screen-time? How many 'family time' nights are spent in front of the TV?

Most of us spend a significant amount of screen time dedicated to work or school as a baseline. The reason this is important is that we don't even need to be having fun or achieving anything for our brains to secrete dopamine. The very frequencies of light that a screen emits are stimuli. Any type of screen is building up your resistance.

Like any other addiction, a chemical imbalance in your brain leads to psychological issues. In this case, being resistant to a happiness indicator can be a contributing factor towards mental illnesses like depression and bipolar disorder. Can you see that you may get depressed if you successfully hit your personal goals but your brain doesn't register your achievements? It's elementary, dear Watson: mess around with the happiness knob and it may cause you to feel unhappy.

One last thing to note, as you decrease your dopamine supply, your cells regenerate their sensitivity. Just as your resistance gradually builds, so too does it drop. What this means is that the less screen-time you get, the more enjoyment per minute your brain gets from screen-time! It is a win-win, the only thing we need to overcome is the human tendency towards addictive behavior.

That might not seem like a simple task. So, where should you start?

There are groups you can join that focus solely on your problems, and it's always just a question away to figure out whether or not one of them is run close to your home. Many addiction-related support groups focus on drugs particularly, but some are opening up their doors to people with tech addictions as well. Will they even be able to relate to your experience? I don't know, could a fellow addict relate to a deterioration of personal relationships and disconnection to others; mood swings; obsessive compulsions; doing things they would never normally do in a healthy mind frame; escapism; self-victimizing and/or abusive internal dialogue? I think they may notice that your fix is different but your problem is the same. No two individuals have the same life experiences, but there is vast common ground. This is the beauty of support groups and why they work so well. Plus, in this day and age, you will likely find a *Gamers Anonymous* (or the like) close by.

At the very least, we will be covering a step-by-step model to run a successful smartphone-restricted day. There is a brilliant slogan used by *Alcoholics Anonymous:* "just for today." This is simple yet fundamental. A recovering addict builds a 10-year career of continuous sobriety one day at a time. There is no other way than conquering the day - every day. It may sound silly, but there is no being sober tomorrow today. There is only being sober today until it becomes a 'sober yesterday.' When you wake up in the morning, you only need to do what is right for you today. A problem that arises in trying to do more is that you will become mentally taxed by attempting to be '10 years improved' in one day. It doesn't work that way. Don't worry about tomorrow, it will be 'today' by the time you can do anything about it: all you need to do is the best you can, just for today.

One final pitfall that those in recovery tend to fall into is backsliding. It is too easy to have a month of doing well under your belt and then to slide back into your previous routine. It happens. Usually, it's caused by engaging in this thought process on a day that you miss your goals: "I missed my goals today, so I failed. I failed, therefore I am a failure. I have proven myself as a failure, therefore I am useless. Because I am a failure and useless, this process cannot work for me, therefore I give up." There will be days that you don't do as well as you would have hoped. It happens, don't get discouraged. There will be days that you may completely derail. That's ok. No one is perfect, and you don't need a perfect record for this process to work. You need courage and perseverance. Courage to weather the bad days and to wake up the next morning with the attitude that it is a new day and you will do your best, just for that day...and then the next, in its own time. Perseverance comes in when you miss your targets, when you don't follow the plan, but still, choose that the process is worth it. Let the prospect of meaningful relationships and the ability to experience happiness, joy, and achievement motivate you. In the end, following a good plan is better than the perfect plan you don't follow, that would be the same as having no plan at all.

A final lesson, you will pay for the life you lead. Like in the old tale of *The Pied Piper*: you can pay now (in hard work and dedication), or have the cost taken from you (in the form of regret) later. Either way, you will have to pay something towards having today at your disposal. If you are young, it would be very worthwhile to sit down with someone you admire and respect to ask them about regret. It is one of life's most cruel lessons to learn for yourself, better to learn from someone else's mistakes. Psychologists around the world have waiting rooms full of regretful people - don't be one of them, for your own sake.

Chapter 2:

Wolves at the Door

Before we go much further, I want to point out the grotesque elephant in the room: online predators. Being a parent, it horrifies me to realize the age that most young children have access to the internet and the types of predators that swim the World Wide Web. Hollywood does a decent job of educating the public on the sometimes fatal consequences of giving children access to the internet. The problem is that far too many parents are either not interested in the 'Crime Drama' or 'Thriller' genre, or they simply lack the gall to stomach the horrific truth.

Imagine this for a moment: your 9-year-old daughter makes a friend online. It may be someone mommy and daddy would like her talking to, but her new friend convinces her to keep it a secret. Late one night her friend visits, as planned, once mommy and daddy are asleep. She goes downstairs and unlocks the door. Her face is then only ever seen on a milk carton thereafter. The end.

It is scary that the average teenager knows more about parental protection software than most parents. They know that if it can be turned on, it can be turned off. Kids have been born into this digital world; just like they learn how to lie about what happened to the cookie jar, they learn how to cover their online tracks. The problem is that parents are far savvier about cookie jars than a browser's cookie cache. If you don't know what a browser's cookie is, then I am sure you get my point. Google knows all! It can tell a child anything they want to know about subverting child-protection measures, using *incognito* mode, or 'tunneling' through a firewall or software by using a proxy. If this is sounding like a foreign language to you, then there's a good chance anyone under the age of 20 may know more about the internet than you.

As if that wasn't bad enough, most adult sites are legally obliged to have an age verification protocol in place. Unfortunately, the average pornography site has a pop-up with two buttons: "I am not 18 (Go Back)," and, "I am +18 Years Old (Let Me In!)." That is it. No second step, no credit card details to be entered. Not so much as a specific birth date request. Two buttons stand between your child and what ought to happen behind closed doors. Some material out there would make *50 Shades of Grey* look like *Teletubbies*.

Do some digging, have there been 'mutually consensual statutory' cases at your local elementary school? Yes, the kids of today are 'trying things out' at unprecedented young ages. There is simply too much exposure to sex for children these days. Waiting until your child is 16 to have 'the talk' is probably too late. If you watch the TV show *Catfish*, you may notice that the 21-year-old imposter that the presenters confront about a particular incident admits to having begun their escapade 7 years prior. Do the math. A 14-year-old teen had begun a career in online identity fraud. A teenager had the know-how to successfully fool a victim (often multiple individuals) into believing they are someone they were not. Most episodes cover cases that are harmless enough: a bit of reality TV drama, nothing too serious. But some show the 21-year-old boy to really be a 45-year-old man living out of a shed on the wrong side of the tracks.

Money can motivate the wrong crowd to do unspeakable things, we looked at how corporations profit from your electronic addiction in the introduction, but what if it gets worse than that? What if we look at the horrors of human trafficking?

Human trafficking is a thriving worldwide industry. Abductions happen every day. It is enough to make my blood freeze in my veins when I think about a loved one walking along the sidewalk when a black van pulls up. Gone. Never seen again. You might be saying: "That only happens in movies…" Wrong! Screenwriters put that scene into movies because it is believable. It is believable because it is plausible. A child sends a pin-drop to an Insta-buddy. Turns out the Instagram profile is fake! A child goes from Washington State to Washington D.C. overnight, if not

Oslo, Ukraine! I don't know the exact figure, but the methods that I have heard used by these human trafficking rings tell me that people can carry a very high price tag as products. Liam Neeson went viral in his role in *Taken* - it was a horrific portrayal of human trafficking, forced heroin addiction, and sexual abuse. It also could be said to have pulled some of the harder punches - after all, it needed to be bearable to perform well in box office sales.

If you have a thing for the horror genre, try a bit of real-life horror: do some digging into human trafficking and child abductions. The age at which some children fall victim is something to keep you up at night.

As a concerned citizen, it would feel a betrayal of your trust if I was to preach from the mountaintop about the long-term life-restricting effects electronics may have without pointing out the potentially fatal, if not worse, occurrences that could be over in a heartbeat - no second chances. Too much screen time is bad for one's health. Unrestricted and unprotected screen-time can kill.

To Catch a Predator, with Chris Hansen, is a nice mix of TV reality, proactive policing, and facts-of-life education that I would recommend to any parent. I would recommend a PG session with children as well, at the very least, a PG session of MTV's *Catfish.* It is one thing that parents know about the trends and do all they can to prevent opportunities for disaster. But, the fact is that the cat is out of the bag: there is no 'shielding' children of today. Keeping them in the dark is no favor. Gone are the days of childhood innocence. Children of today are too latently exposed to the threats to be safe through ignorance. Unless you live an unplugged lifestyle, the threats are in your child's palm. They will likely face some threats when you are not there, so teach them the hard facts - they need to be able to protect themselves. Somehow "stranger danger" isn't enough for the online arena, a child may not feel threatened when in the safety of their room. They may not see the potential danger behind online interactions. Children are online at school and home, and teens are 'big and smart enough' to know better. If grown adults become victims to online predators regularly you can bet everyone younger could do with the added protection of being made 'savvy' to the threats.

I have worked in collaboration between the Sheriff's office and student counselors to put together material that is informative yet still appropriate for some of the schools in my district. I would recommend seeking out (or setting up) education projects that begin education programs as young as the elementary school years. Many predators are opportunistic, educating potential victims empowers kids and removes the opportunity of becoming 'easy prey.'

Thank you for bearing this disturbing subject with me. I have just one more question for you: through the evolution of our modern, digital, society we find the wolves are at our door, knocking on our phones, will you let them in (even dressed as sheep)? I trust you to do what you need to protect those you love.

Chapter 3:

The '*Terminator Effect*'

As the saying goes, "what doesn't kill you makes you stronger." Electronics don't make you stronger. They could kill you. I am not saying that Arnold is going to zap into your living room and give you a live demonstration from his iconic franchise. I am saying: "technology kills." Okay, correction: our chosen application of technology kills all too often. The fact is that this addiction shares a commonality with most addictions - death. Let's run through a few horror stories, the newspapers and internet are full of plenty more.

One obvious factor related to cyberbullying is the 'cyber' aspect - without social media sites there would be no platform for cyberbullying. It is a harrowing statistic that suicide rates are up 65% in the 'teenage girl' demographic because of smartphone usage and addiction. Never has it been more difficult to convince a young and insecure girl that she is 'enough.' Yours is only one voice against the hundred-of-thousands of Insta-followers and the ReTweeters: the "perfect body" is practically worshiped online in a way that would be impossible in any other area of a post-Women's-Suffrage society.

There is no such thing as the perfect body. Take, for example, those that seek aesthetic augmentative surgery (better known as plastic surgery). What is the "best look"? If celebrity trends are anything to go by, they can't agree. Some women pursue the hourglass figure, going so far as to increase bust and hip volume while removing ribs to unnaturally slim the waist. Some plus-sized models focus on tightening their figures but work very hard to maintain volume. Others pay top-dollar to shed wherever possible to adopt as slim of a figure as possible. There are too many (contrary) standards of perfection for an insecure person to stand a chance at achieving total peer acceptance. That is before we even get onto the 'bullying' part... Social media can be nothing short of brutal !

Another disturbing statistic is that approximately 25% of motor vehicle accidents are caused by phone usage while driving. Think, for a moment, of how many safety precautions for driving are visually based: brake light indicators mean slow-to-a-stop; turn signals caution against unanticipated slowing or stopping of the vehicle in front; jaywalkers are an obvious hazard, and yellow lights mean to monitor the speed of any traffic behind and the space available in front - stop if possible, cross if not. I don't mean to come across as condescending here or anything. Yet, somehow, one out of every four incidents is still caused by our illogical need to be preoccupied with our phones when engaging in a very potentially dangerous activity. In 2018 alone, 2,841 died (directly) due to phone-related distractions; not to mention those who sustained debilitating injuries. How many families have been irrevocably devastated by this perfectly avoidable behavior? 15% of fatal crashes involved the combination of driving and phone usage.

Let's talk about this in a language we all understand: money. What do the math magicians think of these statistics? Well, if premiums are anything to go by, all the added safety features and technology deployed in modern vehicles have been completely mitigated according to this bunch of geniuses. I am not being sarcastic. Actuarial scientists have seen car insurance premiums rise by 10,000%! In layman's terms for every $100 you spend on insurance, you could have been spending $1.00... Call me crazy, but it is obvious to me that we are, quite literally, paying for our collective stupidity and negligence.

Speaking of negligence, fatalities are not restricted to driving. While geo-specific apps (like *Pokemon Go!*) have added safety features such as needing to confirm that the player is not the driver when traveling at relatively high speeds and general warnings about being aware of one's environment while playing. These features are simply not enough. There are the stories like a man walking off a cliff (distracted!) or a woman crossing the street without checking if it was safe to do so (heck, Hollywood has used this one so often it's hard to keep track). The fact is, for all our taming of the wilds, the world is a dangerous place to live in. Freak accidents are one thing, but general negligence is a killer. The fact is that screens are the first suspect when investigating cases of absent-mindedness. Do you remember the 'planking' pandemic, where people (young and old) had sustained serious injury or death in the pursuit of the pictorially documented demonstrations of being stiff as a board in a precarious (and often foolishly dangerous) situation? Then there are the real horror stories like a woman that allowed (yes I am saying "allowed") her three children to drown in a pool right next to her because (you guessed it...) she was too busy on her phone. Pity there is no 'save' or 'restore' button on life.

The level of obsession that we feel towards our addiction is painfully clear when you consider the accounts of the "mysteriously crushed man." The only mystery is how it has come to this: he climbed into a trash compactor looking for his phone. The rest is self-evident. But that was just one case, right? True. But there are too many to count that follow the same theme: a woman that ran back into a burning building to get her phone. Her phone had company in the afterlife, smoke inhalation got her. Or, a girl that grabbed a live connection while on top of a train just to get a selfie, it is shocking; excuse the pun.

You do not need all these examples, do you? You have seen, if not through personal experience, close-calls, right? Just watch people descend into the subway, guardian angels are working overtime keeping the average American alive. I look around and think to myself: "I never need to re-watch *Idiocracy*, it is happening around me every day." We care more about Tweets than we do staying alive until tomorrow, or at least that is the story our actions tell.

Let me reiterate: I am all for technology! We take for granted the functionality that I could not have dreamed of as a child watching Sci-Fi movies. The problem is us, or rather, our choices: we choose to be obsessed, addicted, and irresponsible. You can get a new phone, I promise there are thousands in production as we speak! You do not respawn or get any do-overs. We are so concentrated on escaping life that we often take the permanent approach; intentionally or not.

Do you need more proof? Just Google all the stories of individuals that have lost their jobs because they are unable to be productive members of an organization with a screen in the room. Our obsessive choices cost livelihoods, life satisfaction, and lives. The pitfall of smartphones, in no small part, lies in the beauty of their versatility; you can do just about anything on your phone nowadays! At the end of the day, when one emerges from their social media, pornography, or gaming addiction to find that they have done nothing with the last year of their life do you think they will: a) pull up their socks and make up the lost ground; or, b) feel depressed and dive back into a digital world intentionally designed to make them forget about their (self-induced and ever-growing) problems? I admit, there will be a few people picking 'a,' but let's face it most of us need help to avoid going the 'b'-route.

Let's get definitive, in the next chapter we will go through some tests - I hope you studied. The fact is: humans love the game of 'denial.' We are addictive by nature and often excuse it. Even a bodybuilder leverages our habit-building (a.k.a. addictive behavior) to push their bodies through extreme discomfort to reach their '#BodyImageGoals,' yet we do not see their obsessive nature as a bad thing when it is used constructively. Moderation is the aim of the game, so that being said, being the size of a house and having a heart that will attack you in a year is something to be avoided as well.

I am telling you this because if you find you are very addicted as illustrated in the following test scores there is still hope for you. You could be in possession of the best secret weapon against mediocrity you could ever dream of having - just learn to get obsessed about things that make you feel good about who you see in the mirror. If nothing else, learn the coding behind your favorite games or apps - that is where the money is and it follows the saying: "do what you love [in moderation]." When it becomes 'work' you will be more inclined to take a decent amount of breaks. I am preaching 'restriction' not 'elimination' here. Use technology, don't get used by it.

Chapter 4:

The Test

Let's put aside the doom and gloom that can result from smartphone and internet addiction to figure out if you are affected. We will run through a few questions that will tell you how affected you are, or you can take it on behalf of your loved one. These questions will point you in the right direction but feel free to improvise your own. Here is the quick test:

1. Do you check your phone first thing in the morning, at noon, and night?

2. Do you fall asleep with your phone inches away, or even in your hand sometimes?

3. Are you worried or nervous if you haven't been able to check your phone all day?

4. Do you wander on your phone aimlessly for hours on end?

5. Do you spend more time on your phone than you do with actual friends or family (face-to-face)?

6. Is your phone the first thing you pick up when you're bored?

7. Do you start freaking out if your phone battery is about to run out?

8. Do you feel left out or nervous to get it back in your hand?

9. Are you depressed when you go somewhere and there's no cell service?

10. Do friends and family tell you to put your phone down a lot?

11. Have you contemplated cutting your cell phone use?

12. Do you take your phone to the bathroom with you every day?

13. Do you text or call people in the same house as you?

14. Do you use your phone while eating most of your daily meals?

15. Do you often lose track of time while on your phone?

Okay, so you didn't need to study, and it is not much of a personality test. The answers you gave are pretty self-evident. The real purpose behind asking was to draw your attention to the 'normal' behaviors you may exhibit on a daily basis that indicate you may have a problem. The fact is, as an addict, one excuses a lot of tell-tale signs as being 'normal.' Normal and healthy are two very different classifications. Here is an indicator of the level of addition:

- 13-15 Yes's = Addicted Smartphone Junkie

- 10-12 Yes's = Can't Live Without It! Get Out More!

- 7-9 Yes's = Borderline Addict / Need to be careful

- 6 or Below = You're keeping it in moderation

The scores are an indicator, however, any one or two points in excess are enough to disrupt your quality of life. For example points 6 and 15 in excess could be robbing you of your potential and future growth while you are able to maintain decent interpersonal relationships. We feel 'bored' far too quickly, in fact, most of the time it is not boredom at all but an urge for improvement and growth within your life. We can use screens to numb the discomfort of stagnation. However, you feel the uncomfortable sensation of stagnating for a good reason, it is a signal to overcome inertia. In generations past, this psychological signal would trigger wanderlust; persuade us to make new social connections; or pursue a new skill or avenue of learning. 'Boredom' helps us grow, or rather, it is supposed to… Nowadays, reaching Lvl 20 and getting a chest of gems gives us the same level of satisfaction as learning a new guitar riff. So, what's the problem? We are solving the problem, right? I wish it were so, but it isn't for the simple reason that we do not grow as individuals by reaching a new level or league rank. As mentioned previously, these achievements are designed to diminish - fast! The goal is to keep you playing after all. Every single day for as many hours as possible. You are the consumer and if you are not consuming then supply is closing on demand. With the reduction in margin between supply and demand the profit margin decreases. More and more pay-per-view ads are not being viewed.

If gaming is not your vice, you are still not out of the woods. Intimacy is in scarce supply these days because we operate on an ever-increasing superficial level. Social media reprograms our brains to make us believe that we need hundreds, if not thousands, of so-called "friends." The fact is we just end up posting funny memes on like-minded individual's walls only to be rewarded with a sentence or two - most of which are emojis! We are more interested in spreading the media and news related to charitable organizations than actually donating resources or investing time to solve any of the issues. We feel like we have friends. We feel that our efforts are changing society for the better, but the stark truth is that we are squandering our efforts to connect with others and improve the world by finding a creative way to engage with our addiction.

A smoker will tell you that one perk of smoking is that smokers socialize - offering a light is the perfect icebreaker for those who indulge. Cancer and heart disease don't get the memo that you are only a smoker for the social perks. A phone addict will tell you that the COVID-19 virus doesn't know how to surf the web. Depression and obsession don't care what reasons or justifications are given, the addict is still a target. Tragically, this new post-pandemic society is at risk of venerating online migration, there are actual perks, true. But make no mistake: the increased risks are very real.

You might feel a bit cheated by the quality of the test I gave earlier, after all, tests pose a challenge and promise achievement for doing well. Let me not rob you of your opportunity then. You asked for it, even if you didn't. Here it is: "I challenge you!" This is what I call "*The Brick Challenge*": committing to use only a 'brick' for one month. To clarify a 'brick' is a cellphone that belongs to the same generation as the Nokia 3310/5110/6210 or Motorola 300e/6200. The actual model doesn't matter, there are just a few criteria that are satisfied by one feature in particular: internet incapable. If it has a monochrome screen that radiates black if you try touching it, you are on the right track. SMS and calls are all you need, it might sound like being vaulted into a horror film. I bet that A.G. Bell would have had to collect his jaw from the floor if you told him that we would combine the telegraph and his invention and then take away the wires, so it is not so bad.

Okay, so you might need your emails for work or school - we have a workaround. There are apps that are used for parental control or phone addiction that can disable features and apps on your phone. Disable everything that is not absolutely necessary and turn off all notifications in your settings. Next, off with the GPS, WiFi, and mobile data capabilities - fair warning: your VoIP calls won't work, you will have to rely on good-ol'-fashion air-time. This is quickly becoming an honesty exercise; but, it's not me that you will be cheating, if it comes to that, it will be yourself.

If you are able to go without the fundamental features of text and calls, then I double-dare you to go commando! No phone! I tip my hat to you, this is the real cold-turkey approach.

So let's cover the goals of this challenge so that if you need to make an honest exception here or there you know how to keep true to the cause. Primarily, we want to cut out the temptation of the internet - there are just too many possible distractions, especially since you have probably accepted a Google clause entitling them to analyze your activity (and, thus, tailor-make any number of ads and suggestions that ought to be right up your alley). So we are eliminating the bait that will lead you back into hours of screen-time. No YouTube videos - for this period; if you need to know something get a book or ask someone. Interacting with real people is an extremely rewarding process - there is a unique and mutually rewarding relationship that develops between student and mentor. If you are the D.I.Y. type, hit the library. There is a good reason that so many tax dollars are still being invested in the public library system - go find it! As a plus, I am not aware of too many serial-killer biographies involving hanging out at the library, so it is a relatively safe place to make new acquaintances (they tend to be well-read and interesting).

A secondary aim is to give you a hands-on assessment illustrating when you feel the 'itch' to indulge in this addictive behavior. While the questions earlier point you in the right direction, the fact is that we find the easiest person to lie to is ourselves. After all, who would know what you need to hear in order to believe anything better than your own mind? This challenge forces you to come face-to-face with your inner demon of addiction, you can see for yourself what you feel you are missing the most. With a bit of self-reflection, you can identify your triggers: the situations and activities that lead to you picking up your phone. As an obvious example, you need to do some math - your phone has a calculator. Since you are on your phone, why not check that Facebook comment that popped up while number crunching? Four hours later one may find you still on your phone.

The duration is only a guideline. As a rule of thumb, it takes six weeks of completely abstaining from the addiction in order to break the habit. If you can keep up the challenge until you hit six weeks, you will pole vault yourself into a good position on your road to recovery. That said, you may only be up to doing this for a week or two. That is ok. You are looking at a lifetime to gradually improve your quality of life at a pace that is good for you - it goes without saying that the sooner you do this the more benefits you will experience, and the quicker you will notice the improvements. But, back to the AA slogan: just for today. Consistent baby steps are better than a huge leap followed by a massive backslide. This is a marathon, if you need a slow pace because you are so addicted then take your time, but be sure not to fool yourself. So long as you are making progress you are on the right track.

Do not be afraid to let those that care about you know about your challenge, there is no substitute for a good support structure when it comes to conquering addiction, of any type. The first step is to set up a buddy system, get a friend or family member to take the challenge with you. If your whole family unit is on board, all the better. Having peer support works exactly the same way as the notorious 'peer pressure' factor. If your whole social circle or household is going through the same experience, then you will reap the benefits of being able to use the new culture to encourage your efforts. Sit down and have a chat with your buddy, or circle, at regular intervals to discuss the temptations that everyone is facing and to congratulate each other on sticking to the program. I cannot stress the motivational value of an earnest "well done" enough. I would be very surprised if a month goes by without a backslide - that is understandable - especially if there are several people involved. In these situations encouragement is better than criticism: to borrow from an old saying, "it is the rain, not the thunder, that helps the flower grow."

If you find this is an impossible task, fine, go for a 'soft' approach. Limit your screen time to a very small, pre-determined, window of time and journal it. Keep a written record of exactly how long you 'paused' the challenge and what you did. Also, include how you felt when you 'needed' to break with the challenge and how you felt during your screen-time. Lastly, include how you felt afterward and how you felt about yourself (pre, during, and after). What I mean by that last bit is: what did you think of yourself as a person - disappointed, excused, fed-up? Understanding your psychology and emotional motivations during your weakest moments will help you grow stronger and develop better self-discipline.

We will cover this in more detail later, but for now, let's just say that addiction (on a mental level) is a mindset. You can step back from it and pick up the reins or you can lean into it and be pulled into the addiction. Think of a whirlpool, on the outer reaches the pull is relatively weak with a wide circle and slow speed. At the center of the whirlpool, the pull is inescapable with a small circumference and hellish speed - just before you get sucked under. There is a gradual transition between the two extremes, if you can break away from the pull early on then recovery is exponentially easier than if you are almost at the point of having your head underwater.

The effort of resisting the urge to lean into the addiction is half the battle won already.

Let's recap on the material here, this is where the rubber begins to hit the road as far as correcting the problem goes. Set a baseline of where you think you are with the questions first listed. Next, test out your baseline assessment against the practical challenge: "*The Brick Challenge*" - feel free to throw the brick idea out the window and go cold-turkey. Here you will be looking to actively note and resist your personal triggers as well as cutting out the major escalation factor: the internet. Set up a buddy system or support network, include them in your challenge if possible. I would also suggest keeping a journal of your experience, if you do not already do so, to track your own personal evolution through the process - whether you take the 'soft' option or not.

Honestly, this challenge is a tall order, if you are just about to get sucked down it may seem impossible. Or, you might find the vagueness is daunting. Autonomy is a very intimidating prospect for some, it's all good. In the next chapter, I will go through another, far more structured routine for you to follow step-by-step. We are all different, no matter which way works for you, the important thing is that you find a method to improve your life.

Chapter 5:

It's Time For a Change.

Here's How to Do It...

Like all addictions, the addiction one has to their smartphone is a tough one to break. The first few days will be the toughest to go through. This is because your brain will be missing those small and consistent dopamine hits that it's come to rely on to be normal. Without your smartphone to fuel those hits, it'll be normal for you to feel down.

Several therapy methods and step programs have proven to be successful in combating addictive behavior, one of the most popular ones is the substitution method. How this works for smartphone addiction is by scheduling screen-time and sticking to that schedule. If nothing else is scheduled, then we may feel a greater temptation to fill our free time with screen-time than we would if we had something to do. Have you noticed this trend, having nothing to do means it's time to check your phone?

We have covered *The Brick Challenge* in the last chapter - this is an abstinence approach. This is the restriction approach and I will be sharing a schedule with you. It will be as easy as allocating screen time and sticking to only having screen time during these restricted allocations.

Day 1:

Wake up, and turn off all notifications for your big time waster apps for three hours. YouTube, Tiktok, phone games - anything that makes you pick up your phone and waste your morning time.

Try to keep your phone out of your hand as much as possible during this time. The three hours you've freed up for yourself should be spent doing productive things! Use the first day to plan out a morning routine that doesn't incorporate your phone. Some examples of things you could do are planning out your day or week, or taking some extra time to do your morning hygiene routines. You should consider going outside as well!

One of the best substitutes to kick addictions is exercise. Like smartphones, exercise also releases dopamine in our bodies. Plus, it'll keep you healthier. You don't have to do anything highly demanding, either. No one's asking you to become a powerlifter overnight. Rather, have a nice morning walk - or a jog, even a bike ride, if you like those better!

Cook for yourself and, while you're eating, you should do nothing but eat. The relationship that people have with food is often laden with other distractions. You'll see people reading, watching television, or going on their smartphones while they eat. Oftentimes, people eat this way not because they're actually hungry. If you focus on your food while you're eating and nothing else but the action of eating it, you will feel fuller as a result. The pleasure of your food carries you through and gives its own dopamine hit. This will help you develop a healthy relationship with your body and its needs, as well.

Fill your time as best as you can, and make plans to continue filling your time throughout the next couple of days. The process will get more difficult as the days go on and your brain demands the consistent dopamine hit it's missing from you ignoring your phone. Come into this with the expectation that you're going to be fighting for control of your brain.

Day 2:

We're going another step further today. In addition to the big time waster apps of yesterday, you'll also be turning off your social media apps. Twitter, Instagram, Facebook, and MySpace (if you're retro) all fall into this category. Schedule those notifications to be off from the time that you wake up till six hours from then.

What you want to cut out are the notifications that someone's liked or commented on a post you may have made. Or notifications of posts you may be interested in. Social media works in such a way that it appeals to what it thinks you like based on the things you've read or responded to. It's an algorithm that intentionally seeks to draw you in - every second you spend on the platform is money lining the company's pockets. Social media companies make their living on you wasting your time on their platforms.

Don't give in. This will be tougher than not spending time on video or game apps. Naturally, humans have the desire for other peoples' attention and affirmation. That's why social media is as addicting as it is. With social media, you're in constant contact with people who will respond to your posts and interact with you. It's a convenient way to socialize without ever actually having to see your friends - but how happy does it make you to be sitting on your couch scrolling, really?

Use this day to spend time with friends, family, or doing something just for you to pamper yourself. There's nothing like genuine human contact to get over smartphone addiction! Whatever you do, make sure it's with others. In truth, what you seek from your social media accounts is the connection you feel to others.

That's why it's so hard to put your phone down, after all.

If you have trouble with reaching out to people to interact with them directly, local hang outs and club meetings are a good alternative. There are locally run clubs you can find anywhere that focuses on peoples' hobbies and heritages. You should look into picking up one of these. They're a great way to make friends that share your interests, and to interact with people in person. These places are always open to new people, so don't worry about being the new person there. You will most assuredly be welcomed!

If, for anxiety reasons, this makes you nervous, there are options to go out in public and interact with others indirectly. Go to a coffee shop or any calm atmosphere where you can focus on doing something non-screen-related for yourself. One great example of this is people watching. There's a pleasurable quality for some to be a fly on the wall. If that's more your speed, that's totally okay.

Casually observe as people go about their business from a peaceful spot - a bench in a park, for instance. If you like animals, you can go to a dog park and watch the dogs play. In these environments, you may even be allowed to sit in the dog park. In this case, it's more than likely you'll get some attention from the dogs - which will allow you to converse with their owners by proxy. If you're socially anxious, the dogs can act as a sort of filter for you to interact with others from a distance. This will help you get more comfortable in social settings in the long run.

If you prefer a more quiet experience, consider journaling or drawing with a pen and paper at your local cafe. People will be less likely to bother you if you're busy doing something. However, you may notice regular customers paying more attention to you the longer you come in. You'll develop a sense of community with these people even without talking to them much, which is part of the beauty of local cafes. You'll gain recognition from the staff as well, who might even have your order ready the moment you walk in at some locations.

Whatever you choose to do, be present for the experience. Allow yourself the opportunity to enjoy what you're doing without the distraction of a phone. With time, you'll find that your knee-jerk reaction to pick up your phone will diminish.

Day 3:

Today, you're going to take it up a notch. You'll bump up your notification blocking time to ten hours, which will probably be a step you're on for quite a while before you start to find that your need to pick up the phone is weakening. That's why time management and planning your day from day one is paramount to your success.

Ten hours is quite a bit of time, but when broken down into chunks, quite manageable. Keeping daily planners helps you break up the time you have in a day to do things that should be done as well as things you would like to do. Divide your time between chores at home, practicing good hygiene, your hobbies, your crafts, and work. You should also plan to spend some time with your friends and family, especially if this falls outside of your ten-hour allotment of notification blocking. It's easier for you to ignore your phone when there are other people around to distract you.

If you don't have a job to fill that time, work on applying to jobs. Work on a resume at a local library (easy printer access!) and then peruse your area. The places you frequent may even be hiring. If you love the businesses you're a customer with, then it's likely that you'll be passionate about working there as well. Employers fall in love with applicants who really care about the business and what they do, and they'll already know about you from interacting with you when you've gone to their business! There are tons of jobs handed out to people nowadays who may not necessarily have the experience of working in those environments solely because they're a part of the community that business has fostered.

With a good strategy, this step should be a breeze for you. You already have the experience from the last couple of days of being present with your community and yourself, so being without your smartphone for that long won't really bother you as long as you keep busy.

At the end of the day, look over the apps you have that you don't need. Think about how you've felt over the last couple of days and how socially and personally fulfilled you were by what you were doing. The hit from live real-life face-to-face interaction is sure to outweigh what your applications have been making you feel, right?

It's time to delete them. Get the games off your phone entirely, especially while you're recovering from this addiction. Look through your friend lists and unfriend people who you don't actually talk to, or who don't really even know you - especially if you frequent their posts. In addiction recovery, it's often the case that people who suffer from those conditions will have to cut off all contact they have with the people and places that enabled them to become users in the first place. Your smartphone is the same way, in that regard. While it's not always possible to part with a smartphone for work reasons, you should strive to erase as much of the temptation as you can. Keep your phone off of you as much as possible - in a drawer in another room, anywhere as long as it's away from you.

This part is frightening for all people who experience addiction. When you get accustomed to living a certain way, it's difficult to find new ways to fill up your time. That's where your personality can make all the difference for you.

Once you've made it through day three, and developed a good routine for yourself, congratulate yourself. What you're doing is no easy task.

Day 4:

Today, you'll wake up and you'll turn off all your notifications for the whole day. You'll continue to weed out the people you're following on the internet, who you haven't seen or talked to for months. You'll probably find a lot of people fall into this category.

Then you're going to go be social! Spend as much time today with others as you possibly can, as it's very likely you're feeling like you're very disconnected from others at this point. That's a normal feeling as you're recovering from smartphone addiction, so fill up your time with your friends and family. Fit this into your routine as best as you can.

Day 5:

For today, it's time to look at your social media again. That small handful of people you have left on your socials? Read through their posts. Look at all their pictures and get to know these people again. Have you appreciated the bond you have with these people as much as you should have been?

The chances are, probably not. So now it's time to do just that: appreciate people. Reach out to your friends and family and remind them of your love for them. Comment on their posts, engage with them on social media. Make plans with them. Internally, make plans to deepen your relationships with these people and to make new memories with them.

This will likely take up a great chunk of your time today and don't sweat it. This is a healthy way to interact with your loved ones, and you're making plans to do more with them as the days go on. You're weaning yourself off your smartphone, not cutting it out cold turkey.

Prepare yourself to have another great day of progress tomorrow!

Day 6:

Turn your notifications on today! Today is big. You're going to want to collect all your friend's and family's phone numbers, email addresses, and birthdays (if you don't already know them). Give them phone calls and let them know about what you're doing to recover from your smartphone addiction, and how you'd like them to get a hold of you going forward.

It's likely all of them have had similar thoughts as you with regards to breaking their dependency on their smartphones. This is a great thing, as you can support one another during this process.

After that, you don't need anything else. Get back on that routine and do what you've been doing with your phone - ignoring it for greater things.

Day 7:

Now that you have all your phone numbers, emails, and birthdays, it's time to take the jump. If you need to make a few more phone calls to let everyone know you're breaking an addiction, do that! When you're done with this, you will have all the information you need to keep in contact with your loved ones.

It's time to delete your social accounts. Uninstall those apps, get rid of them.

When you've finally put down the smartphone on day seven, you'll have plenty of time to explore yourself and the world around you. There was a time before when people would wake up, and that's all they did! They didn't reach for their smartphone. They didn't scroll through the news only to fill up their minds with terrible, depressing things on a daily basis.

Curiosity killed the cat, as they say. In terms of a smartphone addiction, what I mean by this is that you have a desire to know things, and that will hurt you in the long run. It's difficult to go looking through the news and social media without finding something upsetting that's going to take up mental space for you, whether you realize it or not. Maybe your friends are vague-posting depressing things, maybe that's incredibly dark and dreadful news.

While being aware of your social environment and the changes that are happening to it is certainly not bad in and of itself, it does have a lasting effect on our psyche to be constantly battered with bad news. Nowadays, people are tired. Depression rates are higher than they've ever been - a reality that gets more and more drastic with every passing year. People forget to spend time, in person, with the people that they love the most - families, friends. Without being aware of it, you've allowed yourself to get so filled up on the bad that there's no room, or energy, for all the good that life has to offer.

At some point, you need to be able to tell yourself, "No. I need a break from the world." Often, people who are recovering from a smartphone addiction only became addicted in the first place out of a misbegotten attempt to stay in touch with everyone. Similarly, things seem so much more urgent now that smartphones and the internet have made our social lives instant.

The truth of the matter is that the world is going to have bad news and most of the time there's nothing you can do about it, regardless of you knowing or not. Your friends are going to have hard days that you can't be there for. That video game you were playing doesn't need to be logged into on a daily basis for you to feel like you're reaping the benefit of playing a game. You don't need to scroll constantly, or at all. You don't need to message people right away to keep in contact with them and see how they're doing.

People even fifteen years ago didn't have smartphones nearly as advanced as they are today. Smartphones are incredibly new, and while they are useful tools, they should not be allowed to rule your life.

To put this into perspective, a popular online content production company called Rooster Teeth released a documentary called *Connected* which follows two of their talents - Barbara Dunkelman and Blaine Gibson on a journey to live without a smartphone for a month (Burns et. al, 2016). During the documentary, the two found they had huge amounts of time lulls in their day and dependencies on their smartphones that they hadn't even thought of.

At the end of the month, the two managed to find new hobbies and new ways to meet people for dates. They also figured out how to get around their city without the use of a smartphone's GPS capabilities.

While it is ironic that a company like Rooster Teeth, which banks on its audience's dependency on the internet, created a documentary like this is truly palpable, the messaging behind the film is important and increasingly relevant. Blaine Gibson and Barbara Dunkelman are two incredibly talented and popular individuals, to be sure. On their month-long journey of smartphone abstinence, however, the two managed to cultivate other ways to express their creativity as well as ways to connect with other people in real, tangible ways.

The possibilities of attaining the same type of freedom that they experienced are as likely or more for you, should you be willing to put the time and effort into exploring yourself and the community in which you live. Maybe you even go beyond your immediate personal community to find and explore subcultures or other communities that you may not have appreciated the presence of in your town. Maybe you spend your time taking up new creative pursuits and discovering ways to express your emotions and thoughts in the same ways that the great artists of history could.

When you give yourself the time to explore, the time to think and be present in your internal world, you open yourself up to your own potential. How could you have ever known there was a painter in you if you were too busy watching other people painting on YouTube? How could you have ever known that you deeply love philosophy when all you've done is immerse yourself in the thoughts of others without ever considering for yourself? What if there's something that you do enjoy that you don't appreciate nearly as much as you should because you've broken up the time you do it with the presence and distraction of the internet?

Keep Going

From the third day, carry on with your new habits for a week. Keep in touch with yourself every single day, and monitor how you feel. Be brutally honest with yourself as the days go on and change the schedule as you need to keep busy, and most importantly, inspired.

You'll find that you will need to develop new coping mechanisms while you overcome your smartphone addiction. For every person struggling with addiction, this is no straight path. When you're away from your phone, you should expect that trying new things will not always result in immediate success and fulfillment. Sometimes things just aren't right for you, or maybe it's not the right time to be doing them.

Or maybe it's not the right environment. Changing your environment up has an interesting effect on your mentality. When you go to new places, their respective atmospheres tend to change how you behave in general - this can also leave impressions on how we think and feel in those places and leaving them, especially if they're totally new experiences.

For this week, you might find it helpful to set small daily goals for yourself. On a piece of paper, write down your dreams and aspirations for your life, and also write down the little things you'd like to accomplish that day. Start learning a new language, maybe. You could even go about reading a few chapters of a book or doing ten push-ups or anything that you might be interested in at all. Start small, and work your way up to build yourself up.

Another thing you should do is write yourself messages to remind yourself why you're doing what you're doing, as well as kind encouragements to yourself to keep your momentum up. Leave yourself a few notes around your home with motivational messages. Write down the things you love about yourself and your life! Remind yourself of the good as much as you possibly can.

You're going to change, and you're going to grow. That's the important part of this whole ordeal! You'll be stepping outside of your comfort zone and learning new, exciting things about yourself every day. You're going to see where your boundaries are with things you've never thought of doing, and you're going to find ways to tell those boundaries to shove it because you're going to do the thing whether they exist or not. You will develop a resilience and constitution you never even realized you could have.

By the end of the week, you'll find there was a lot on your smartphone that you never really needed. You convinced yourself that you needed your Google Calendar to remind you of what's happening next, but without all the distractions of your smartphone, you'll realize you have more mental space to remember those events for yourself. You'll find that you aren't alone when you're not constantly connected and that the fruits of a genuine in-person interaction are higher quality than any of the micro-interactions you had online.

But it's not going to be easy. Nothing worth doing in this life is easy. No one was ever born a champion, they were forged into one with determination and iron resolve.

The process of recovery is difficult for all people with addictions, smartphone addiction included. As you continue with this process and cut the social media and screen time from your life, you will find that you feel better and better with every day. After cutting out the smartphone, you'll have made space for the rest of life to take its place. Fill your heart with the joys you experience in your day-to-day, and be present for every single moment!

The most important part of this process is learning how to be alone without feeling lonely. You're amazing, and you should love the time that you spend with yourself in your imagination and thoughts.

Chapter 6:

Stepping Back

Reflecting on the whirlpool metaphor: in the outer reaches it is easy to keep one's bearings as one circles gradually around the circumference; but, close to the center, the frequency becomes disorientating. Frequency is a key factor in keeping an addictive behavior in check. The more frequent your thoughts and actions concerning a particular behavior are, the more and more frequent the behaviors become. It is a vicious cycle! 'Obsession' is simply a level of higher frequency; a point where thinking about anything else is a second priority.

In this chapter, we are going to cover a principle that is used in areas as modern as cognitive psychotherapy and spanning back to the traditions of Zen Buddhism and Taoism - though I would bet it has roots far further back than that. It harnesses a fundamental function of the mind in a way that overcomes the natural spiral of obsession progression. The ancients used to refer to the process as 'dropping' the unwanted mental baggage. This is a very hard process for most to wrap their minds around because it is so simple. We tend to attempt to over-think this process, try to get to the hidden secret mechanics behind it. The hidden secret is that there is no secret. Complications arise from trying to 'understand' what happens. It is self-evident. It is simple. For that very reason, it seems impossible to implement for a great many.

The process is also described as 'watching' the thoughts concerning a potentially obsessive behavior. The usual flow is to think and then to act. We do this instinctively. Try moving your finger; you mentally set the intention to move and your body responds automatically. If you want a cup of tea, you may find yourself switching on the kettle by the time you become aware of your desire for tea. Then again, you may never become aware of the desire behind the making of the tea - you simply make the tea and drink it.

As humans, we have an amazing autopilot system. Take our nervous system, for example: half of our nerves are under our direct control, but there is another part that is completely automated. If your hand is electrocuted, it uncontrollably clenches. When was the last time you remembered to make your heart beat? Even our breathing (a voluntary system) operates on autopilot by default. You can choose to hyperventilate, or to hold your breath, but once you pass out your body goes back to a sustainable rhythm. Our routines are much the same: we can choose to do certain activities but a great deal happens on its own. When eating breakfast, you can choose to chew every bite fifty-two times and actively savor every mouthful. Or, you can pick up the spoon or fork almost automatically and watch a YouTube video until your food is finished. If it wasn't so commonplace, this ability might even strike you like magic. You can breathe and swallow while being quite unaware of the process, all without choking. Again, this is a marvelous feat, but we take it for granted.

The reason I bring this tendency towards automation to your attention is to point out that obsessive and addictive behavior use the same principle. We are quite literally compelled to feel and act in a certain way because it follows an established pattern. We 'must' check the latest feeds on our favorite channels when we wake up because we have done this so often before. There is little else that anchors this behavior except for the ones that we place; yes we also crave our screen-time dopamine fix, but that is a sort of automation of its own too. We need a certain level of drug or hormone in our system because we have consistently provided this baseline.

The method described by ancient mystic traditions is the same process that cognitive therapy employs. Just don't do what you feel compelled to do. It takes a strong will to ignore your instinct, but it is that simple. I am including this method because, while some of you may find this useless, there are those select few that need this (and only this chapter) to go from addict to fully functional. It takes inner strength, but this culture that we live in does not just prey on those with above-average addictive tendencies.

The key here is your focus, or rather, cultivating your focus. Our technological addiction takes the driving seat by pushing any other focus we may have to one side. Or, by incorporating the other focuses into its own system. For example, you have a basic human need to socialize - Maslow pointed this out, it's featured on his hierarchy. The electronic addiction becomes stronger through you anchoring (or attaching) this need to an electronic medium like Twitter or Facebook. You can weaken the anchor by avoiding the electronic medium and satisfying your need to socialize through face-to-face interactions.

Every time you successfully distance yourself from a process that had been automated, your brain starts to dissociate from the automated model it had relied upon and starts to learn a new automation. In doing so, you are swimming back out to the outer reaches of our metaphoric whirlpool. We are weakening the link and, thus, we weaken the strength of the next inclination. Your first "no" is the hardest, each after will become easier and easier.

The cold-turkey style challenge and our structured routine are in place for individuals that need those approaches (it is okay if you do). This method can be used either before or on its own. The method simply consists of becoming aware of the urge as it happens. This would usually be indicated by the involuntary and automated outstretching of your hand for a screen. It is at this point that we usually direct our focus to the screen and do what we have always done, reinforcing the automated process that we have already built from our past decisions. You do still have a choice, though. You can pause at that moment and ask, "Do I want to do this, and if so, why?" You could find you need to send an important message to your boss - that is a productive and legitimate reason. Go ahead, type your email. Done. You have just successfully used technology like the servant that it is meant to be. You could find that you are simply 'bored' and that scrolling on Instagram is the goal. Why? What good will it do for you? If you have a friend in mind that is two states over whom you are genuinely interested in contacting, then that could be a legitimate reason. I say 'could be' because that answer may only come to you when you do some self-interrogation; in which case you would probably not have messaged that person over the two hours of mindless Insta-zombie time your question just interrupted. See what I mean here? Is it that person that you really wanted to talk to, or is that an excuse for screen-time?

By simply bringing your focus to the tasks you leave to your autopilot, you might find that your autopilot is not trying to build the best life for the future version of yourself, it is simply trying to keep you alive. That is exactly how the subconscious mind works - it follows the principles of, 'keep doing what you have always done and you will keep getting what you have already got.' It is no hidden genius that will make your life better, it is a safety feature. Have you ever noticed that you may be daydreaming or deep in thought but then an external event such as a loud noise snaps you back to reality? That is your autopilot shutting down and handing the controls back over to your conscious mind because "things are no longer how they have always been... Danger!" Your conscious mind then needs to assess if you are still safe or if immediate action is needed to stay alive.

Your subconscious autopilot is also not too aware of anything in the future. It runs on protocols, similar to computer coding, which reason like this: "I spent 8 hours on YouTube yesterday and I survived. An additional 12 hours of Crushing and Clashing and I survived." The fact that sleep deprivation may lead to you stepping out in front of a school bus because you didn't think about checking if it was safe is not a part of its equation. Our autopilot is a reactive and reflective program, it is very limited in its predictive abilities.

So, when you catch your hand reaching for your phone and ask what it is doing, take a step back and ask another question: "what will the me of tomorrow, or next year, think about my behavior today?"

Disengaging from your autopilot already weakens your addiction, being able to step back and choose to not continue that behavior is conquering the addiction. For a smoker, in order to quit, all they have to do is nothing, just avoid smoking. When they feel like smoking and leave it at that, no cigarette lit, they become a non-smoker or ex-smoker. It is that simple, right? But it does take considerable strength of will to do so. You can build your willpower by any means, but one of the best ways is to take up mindfulness meditations. Before there are any misinformed objections, the basic mindfulness meditation practice is non-denominational.

There are several lifestyle benefits to this practice, but the most applicable one is to provide you with the practice for taking a step back, essentially, that is all you do for the most basic form of the practice.

So let's quickly cover a small fact that might hit you like a bombshell: you are not your mind. Before you think that I'm completely crazy, let me clarify: your mind is you, well part of you, much like your heart or thumb. And, much like any organ of yours, your mind is not the whole you. Your mind processes thought and is easily confused with the real you, your consciousness. Think about it, we have been covering questions for you to ask yourself in the previous paragraphs: who is asking and who is answering? It didn't seem crazy when we were stopping to ask: "Why am I doing this?" So, who was asking? Does it seem rational to say that it was your you-ness, your consciousness, that was asking your mind, the aspect of you that processes thought? When you find yourself struggling with an addiction, there are thoughts of why-not-to and the thoughts that argue for doing whatever it is that you are struggling over. It becomes a battle of logic and pseudo-logic: all thoughts.

It is a battle within your mind, trying to fight it on a mental level is to risk casualty.

Have you ever heard the saying: "Don't argue with an idiot: they will drag you down to their level then beat you with experience"? I find it funny but true. I have tried such arguments - no matter what, the fool ends up believing that they have won and I end up with a headache for my efforts. It's not worth it! It is the same with attempting to out-think your mind, you are most likely going to lose. And when you lose, in this case, you will just end up doing the activities that you are addicted to - even if you didn't want to at first, you will. You have all the right reasons to, after all. You have things you want to do in life, and that will drive you forward.

So what is the solution? Well, it lies in not wanting to do something, just don't think about it. Your consciousness is your secret weapon. The trouble with society is that we think that thoughts are the beginning and end of everything. Willpower seems to be something optional. People think that you can exercise it if you can if you want to, and sure it has its perks, but it's not necessary.

Let's run through the theory of the most basic mindfulness meditation. This is enough to: 1) help you stop overthinking your addiction when you find yourself battling with doing the best thing for the future you; and 2) give you a simple and practical method to build willpower. Here it goes:

1. Find a quiet place to sit or lie down, whatever is comfortable

2. Close your eyes

3. Bring your attention to your breathing;

   • inhale to fill your belly

   • let your belly empty as you exhale

4. When a thought enters your mind, and it will:

   • acknowledge the fact there is a thought

   • let it pass, no matter how important or urgent it may seem

   • focus, again, on your in-and-out breathing

That's it. You can count to four or five with your breathing if you'd like. You can hold your in or out breaths, or not. The principle, and thus our aim, is to find one focal point on which to keep our attention for a prolonged period of time. 'Prolonged' is relative; you will find that five minutes is a prolonged time frame once you become aware of the freeway that is your unattended mind.

How is this relevant? Firstly, you can observe the balance of control between your will and mind: every intruding thought is an attempt by your mind to steal focus back over from your will. One thought rolls onto the next, and then the next - mind wins. Secondly, you become aware of the deeper nature of thoughts, so, when you feel the 'itch' to pick up a device you can spot where you are moving from living through willpower into living through autopilot. Lastly, you are getting damn good at not entertaining thoughts when you don't want to - when you feel the urge to succumb to your addiction you already know that there is an 'off switch' and how to flip it.

Let's stop here for a second. You, reader (yes, I see you), fit into one of two categories concerning your ability to turn off your thoughts: you either know exactly what I am talking about (in which case, thank you for bearing with me); or, you think this is all sci-fi. If you are the latter then I have a mini-challenge for you: set your alarm for 5 minutes. We can both agree that you can breathe without thinking about it - so, for this time, just breathe without thinking about it or anything else... Fast forward 5 minutes: welcome to category #1; you are starting to follow what you have been reading, right? Did you notice that you were still around for those periods where you weren't thinking?

As you get better with this technique you will notice that there are two truisms that you can use to overcome your addictive tendencies: mind-over-matter and will-over-mind. The more you exercise your will, the more willpower you will have in every aspect of your life. Okay, now is a good time to admit to a little white lie: I started off by telling you that this section will only work for strong-willed people; the truth is, anyone can use this to become strong-willed - so this is for you, no matter where you are on your path. It is a really fun and relaxing exercise to do with children as well. Having small quiet time breaks on a daily basis adds an extra level to a family's intimacy and connection. Everyone comes together for 15 minutes once a day, plus, if it is a synchronized activity, there are fewer possible distractions.

It will become apparent what is meant by 'dropping' something, like a bad habit, through experiencing these quiet mindfulness sessions. The trick is to drop it and not pick it up again. Just like a smoker that simply does not light another cigarette, ever. 'Quitting' smoking can be extremely hard, but in using a method like this, gently brushing away the thought of lighting a cigarette as they pop up is easy. With consistency and time, a career of recovery is built without ever needing to tackle the task of 'quitting' (which is mentally daunting). If this was football: it is easier to side-step the biggest guy on the field than to try to tackle him. Either way, 'success' is getting past him, around or through. This is one reason why Alcoholics Anonymous just focuses on today. All it takes is not giving in to that one urge in that one moment, the next time is the same.

Chapter 7:

The Effects of Addiction

Once the dust settles, it is easier to see what damage has been done by addictive behavior. Unfortunately, it is very hard to see the full scope of consequences you'll face while in the throes of addiction. Again, back to our whirlpool analogy: when you are spinning round and round at a dizzying pace one loses focus on what is actually happening around them, it is all just a blur with very few things being coherent. Unfortunately, one of these coherent thoughts is the need to satisfy the addiction. One's mind can be obsessed over this thought to the exclusion of most else. Grabbing onto the promise of coherency and clarity, we cling to it like a lifeline - only to find it is dragging us further under. When you just really, really need to check your Facebook page, the thought of socializing by any other means is not appealing. Would you rather spend time watching a boring movie as a family, or 'spend time with real friends' on Facebook?

The more addicted we become to one way of living, the less appealing any alternative becomes in our mind. We get turned off by the way we define the alternative before even considering it - why? Because of the addiction. It is simple, your habitual program in your brain knows what it wants, so the options that are presented to you at the time of making a choice are done in such a way as to eliminate the chance of making the '*wrong*' choice, or rather, choosing to break away from the habit (or addiction).

It seems harmless enough at first glance, but there is a reason people warn against spending time with addicts. Lifelong friends or close relatives are known to steal, even from their own mother, in order to afford substances like alcohol and drugs. You already know this, so what makes a screen addiction any different? The destructive tendencies are not as obvious as stealing to support the addiction (but that is just because the addiction has a cheap running cost once you have provided the initial setup). Think of time and attention as a currency for a moment: does a screen steal time well spent with your loved ones? How often do you talk to your family? Can you remember the last heart-to-heart discussion you had with someone close to you? If you think you can, what was it about? Now sum it up, try to remember the moments that they opened up to you and made themselves vulnerable in order to build a new intimate connection with you. I know that, when I was at my most tech-involved stage, I completely missed the attempts my friends and family made to be truly intimate and vulnerable with me.

How about focusing on time, how much time is spent with friends and family as opposed to on a device? If you were wondering, we are going to classify screen-time with friends or family (like commenting on posts and DMing) as screen time - not as family/friend time. We cloak our addictions with 'legitimacy' in order to fool ourselves into continuing the addiction, this is a universal trait of an addict. Unfortunately, COVID-19 has given us even more reason to avoid *real* interactions with others, but only having screen-time is a recipe for mental disorders. If you share cutlery or coffee mugs with that person, you can afford to socialize with them without any additional risk of infection, plus carrying around a mask and hand sanitizer will put you on the 'very low' side of the risk scale.

It is a horrific fact that most of us will not remember the last time we experienced true intimacy with a person face-to-face. Now, when was the last time you felt you could only adequately express your feelings through text message or voice-note? Tell me if this is familiar: you have a messy argument or huge yelling match and someone storms out (or emotionally shuts off until the other leaves the room); later, be it minutes or hours, there is an exchange of text messages/voice notes that unravel the deep emotions that one had been feeling to the other. Deep empathy is possible through the revelations in a cooled-down tone. Technology is bringing us closer, right? No! This is a destructive dynamic on so many levels.

Firstly, it is understandable that individuals who are not operating on a high E.Q. level will be unable to process their emotions in the heat of the moment while still conveying this analysis in a tone and vocabulary that does not trigger the other's offense-response. And if the first does pull this off to some level of success there is the part about receiving the other's input - being very emotional at the time, a highly emotional response is common. So a disagreement devolves into a conflict far too often. But "all's well that ends well," right?

No. That brings us to the second point. It is natural that after being given space to calm down (and reflect on one's own emotion and the points that had been brought up by the other) we reach a cool clarity and are able to properly articulate these elements in an analytical fashion. This is normal. What is not normal, or rather healthy, is to then associate emotional clarity and, thus, intimacy through digital means. It seems silly that electronics play a role here, but hear me out. Fire is associated with pain when touched - we need to learn this. It is a quick lesson to learn, but there is a reason an infant may reach out to touch a flame: they haven't learned the association yet. Associations are rules that our internal autopilot follows, like computer coding lines. If we repeatedly associate (or experience) intimacy and emotional resolution through digital means and digital means alone, we build the mental rule: "I can only experience beneficial emotions through my phone." Furthermore, we also learn: "Face-to-face emotional interactions are bad. They cause frustration, pain, and are ineffective." Can you see how we may become averse to *real* intimacy and drawn to emotionally opening up over electronic means?

Thirdly, text communication (or voice-note monologuing) is less intimidating, adding an additional attraction to this medium, because there is a greatly reduced risk of rejection. With a lower perceived chance of rejection comes the willingness to open up to a greater degree, emotionally. Again, this is rooted in our neural wiring. When talking face-to-face, we process far more than words. We use the tempo of the speech as a guideline, if the other person begins uncontrollably quickening their tempo, it is an indicator that you may be on thin ice if your goal is to keep the exchange civil. Tone indicates certain aspects as well: have you ever tried being sarcastic via text? It is a real flip of the coin. Pitch is processed by our brain as well. Just like an arrow, once a word is spoken it can not be withdrawn. A four-line text, on the other hand, can be edited for hours before the send button is pressed. While at times this may be a good thing, it calls into question the genuineness of online interaction.

What about our gut feeling when someone lies to us? It isn't all bad: your mother may have told you she "trusts your judgment," while cringing on the inside - all for the sake of allowing you the independence you may need for your own personal growth. She may want to mean it, but she really is faking it until she makes it, so to speak. Over text, you are none the wiser, but in person, you may (if only subconsciously) become aware of the twitch around her eye as she fights back the automatic cringe. You might only consciously register this on a 'gut feeling' level, but you feel something is not genuine about what she told you. This is often how our intuition, or gut feelings, work.

Now to bring it back to our argument scenario, the interaction can get very heated, very quickly when gut feelings and misspoken vocabulary are involved. Just like our whirlpool metaphor, we get caught up in the spin and are unlikely to process everything clearly as things escalate. We make-up over cool-and-calculated texts or voice-notes. When all is said and done we have learned "people bad, phone good."

In this way, our phone robs us of the time and attention with our loved ones through apps and instantly-gratifying distractions. Plus, it robs us of our willingness to attempt intimacy without technology as a middle-man. After all, if someone was to reject you online you could always delete the chat, or just block them. There are so many aspects that reduce our fear of rejection online that we cannot bear the thought of being intimate and open in reality. How many families (the most intimate of all social groups) operate exclusively on a superficial and cordial level? We, as humans, are forgetting what true human connection is… The global depression growth statistics are an empirical indicator of just that.

You might not be hooked on all this talk about intimacy and emotional interconnection. It is very important to me, as a family man and father, but I respect that this may not rank in your top five. That's ok. Let's see what a tech-addiction robs for the lone-wolf type.

How's your mental sharpness? What is 12 multiplied by 13? Got it? Or did you reach for your calculator app? The answer is 156. One method is to do the math: (10x12=120) + (3x12=36) = 156. The second way is to rely on engrained memory, from elementary school "12 x 12 = 144" has been drilled into long term memory: 144 + 12 = 156. An acute mind could have processed one method and verified the answer using the second in the same amount of time that the average person used to type the equation into a calculator. Faster, maybe, if the phone had a lock screen.

I used this example to debunk the most prominent myth: "computers are better than humans." The above problem would have an unaccustomed mind reeling at the realization that the common multiplication table ends at 12 x 12, in which time the calculator spits out the answer – that's proof that calculators are better, right? The truth is that we are becoming worse than computers through lazy habits. The secret to mental sharpness is shared with that of the sharpness of a blade. They both need sharpening on a regular basis. If one allows their mind to become rusty is it any wonder they are out-performed by automation, or anything really?

There are several methods to keep one's mind sharp, but it is important to know what type (or variant) of mental acuity one wishes to cultivate. While it is true that general mental exercise will improve general performance, it is also true that professional athletes in the track disciplines train very differently than those in the field disciplines. Their training schedule further differs when comparing individual events: a marathon runner uses exercises that would not be practical for a short-distance sprinter. Before we focus on the method of getting where you want to go, let's quickly clarify: where do you want to go, what does a 'sharp mind' enable you to do?

At the risk of sounding like a broken record: I am all for the benefits we can get from computers. If calculations are not your thing, that's fine. But the point is that we are allowing the dependency on computers to make us stupid. Can you spell properly? If you are like me, SMS's did a number on your ability to spell, properly punctuate, and use grammar correctly. The cost-savings of sticking to the character limit were way too appealing, at the time, to bother about crossing t's and dotting i's. The youngsters of today don't have that excuse, but auto-correct and predictive text have their own pitfalls.

To borrow a truism from the sayings: "jack of all trades, master of none," it is impossible to be the absolute best at everything you choose to do, but it is important to be good at some things. As humans, we peg a certain value to the things we are good at when we build our self-image. Poor self-esteem is, in no small part, due to the tendency to allow your smartphone to be smarter than you.

Unfortunately, a lot of our mental processing power is wasted on becoming an expert in a certain game's strategies. At the end of the day, being able to hit the global high score in Candy Crush is a useless and expensive experience to build. In college, it is the equivalent of being the undisputed poker champion and failing every academic test. Unless your life's goal is to become a poker world champion, your skill development and what you expect from life are at odds. This is a recipe for an accomplished life. In layman's terms, you are setting yourself up for failure by not becoming good at the skills that are required to achieve the life you wish to have. Thus, you are laboring to be an unhappy version of yourself. Can you see how this ties back into the surge of depression?

How do we deal with depression? Pain-killers or suicide (which is just a final pain-killer). Yes, while some may literally develop a pharmaceutical dependency (or addiction), there are so many other ways to remove the pain of failure from one's mind: alcohol, recreational (i.e. illegal) drugs, food, and (you guessed it!) electronics. Look at the average American: over half of the adult population is obese. Not fat, clinically obese. Back to the case of electronics, it just reinforces our dependency on something that further reduces our ability to turn our life around. They all do. It is a vicious cycle.

A dependency on electronics is both the cause of an unhappy life as well as a coping mechanism for the unhappiness. It never ends!

If all this was not enough, I get furious when I walk into a family home only to find absent-minded adults and their children glued to a TV or a phone. It is a real-life horror story, and it is the new 'norm'!

I cannot even begin to imagine what the next generation will be like. I grew up with only a TV as a temptation. PCs only had solitaire back then. Now, there is no front-page news if a 2-year-old can unlock a phone. Heaven knows what the average 10-year-old has seen on the internet! It is as simple as clicking "Yes, I am +18 (Enter)." The fact is, the web-hosts don't care who is on their sites, most of it is paid for by pay-per-view ads and the sponsor pays for a 10-year-old as much as they do for a 40-year-old. A child has access to stream a movie or documentary with R18 restriction (followed by the entire alphabet's worth of cautionary indicators). Is there any wonder violence in schools is on the rise?

Electronics, and a lack of parental vigilance, have our juvenile detention centers filled with rapists and murders. I am not pushing all the blame onto this one factor, but it is a large contributor to the overall issue. It illustrates unwanted behavior. It allows for poor self-esteem and unrealistic self-expectations. It reduces a family's ability to bond and connect. There is not enough space in a single book to list all the aspects that electronics contribute towards the destruction of innocence in our children. Worse of all, most teenagers know how to cover their digital tracks better than the average adult. How would you feel about sending a child to play in the park that is notorious for having hookers, heroin-junkies, and "ice-cream vans" roaming about at all hours of the day? The fact is that is exactly what the internet is, and most adults are too unexposed or naive to know it!

You can order assassinations with a credit card or PayPal Account on the dark web. Do you, as an adult, know which apps in the Google Play Store or on the Apple App Store are capable of accessing the dark web? Does your child have any of those apps installed on their phone right now? You might find a drug dealer that is happy being paid in Amazon vouchers! The fact is, most adults are blissfully unaware of what kids have access to from their own rooms! Or, did you believe that the dark web was some far-off threat that no child could ever access? It is not hard to access.

You might think this ought to be curbed by the cops, and it is, but these guys are still learning what seems to come naturally to the young tech generation. The FBI have dedicated teams, but it is not enough at this stage.

If your child has a 3D printer, they are capable of downloading a .cad file and watching a YouTube video that will teach them all they need to know about printing a gun! A functioning gun! No serial number, and you can buy all you need from Walmart. It may fire bullets, or it may blow up and take off a hand - either way there is a real danger present.

To make matters worse, you don't even need to buy them a 3D printer, there are DIY videos for building them (it will probably end up looking like a meccano cube with microchips and wires attached). It pains me, but the surest way of keeping everyone safe is to become intimately aware of the real dangers that the internet and tech obsession have brought into our lives. There are a myriad of psychological, emotional, and physical threats that boil down to stomach-churning, blood-freezing, spine-chilling horror before most of us ever realize what is happening.

If the thought of a misguided and angry 14-year-old with access to extremist propaganda and a how-to guide for making homemade explosives from kitchen chemicals doesn't strike fear into your heart, I don't know what will... The fact is, they are both a click away.

You wouldn't set your sheets on fire to warm up on a chilly night, that is obvious. It is time to make obvious the fact that screens are potentially life-ending on so many levels. It is time to see them for the fire they are, this is the new world that we, and those before us, have built for the youth of today. This is our legacy. This is the aftermath.

Chapter 8:

You Are Not Alone

One of my main motivations for writing this book is because I see the degradation of actual society and community. I am concerned about what kind of a world our children will need to face if things continue the way they are headed. We are trading real community for an artificial sense of community. It is an amazing addition, but an inadequate substitute.

It might surprise you, but there is a new fashion trend beginning due to the wide application of blockchain technology: virtual real estate. In a culture dominated by an ever-evolving demand for variety in our financial portfolios, it is only natural that one may want to find a way to sell the same geo-coordinates twice.

However, just like you cannot actually move into any real estate that you may own, there is little substitute for a real social community. Do you spend hours on social media, yet somehow still get the feeling of being lonely on occasion?

It is phenomenal that we can video chat with friends and family half the world away as if they were in the same room as we are. I am confident that our parents would not have dreamed of it as much at our age. While this extended ability to stay in touch with distant loved ones greatly augments our social life, it cannot substitute basic human requirements of actual socializing. Just as we have a human tendency to follow patterns and form habits, or addictions, we also have a herd-animal aspect to our human nature. We need to be around people for our own mental health.

Yes, some more so than others. Introverts expend energy while socializing; and extroverts find that their batteries are being recharged while engaging with others. However, there are very few people that possess the mental fortitude and vocation of living a hermit lifestyle, but these individuals would be the last ones to succumb to any form of tech-addiction, so, for practical reasons, we will leave out the wild survivalists and mountaintop-meditating monks. For the majority of us, solitude breeds loneliness and depression. Take any one of many studies conducted on the negative mental outcomes experienced by people stuck under COVID-19 lockdown conditions. While the measures may have been intended for the greater good, many have succumbed to depression and even suicide as a result of the lockdown knock-on effects. One major factor is the forlorn feeling of being all alone without the comfort of companionship.

It is unfortunate that we can only see the true value of community by the devastation we experience once we are deprived of it. It is a fundamental need that is all too often taken for granted. How aware are you of your need for other people? I may be preaching to the converted, or you may just need to make a list of your most loved memories. How many of these would not be the same if you had been all alone? Just you, no one else. I would hazard a guess that many, if not all, of them would not make your 'best memories' list at all.

Families have a special bond. This bond has formed our history as we know it. Where would we be without the monarchy and oligarchy systems? Maybe no better, possibly no worse; but the world we know would not be as we know it. Only relatively recently has democracy become a political driving force on the international stage - but even in an established bastion of democracy, the constantly recurring incidents of nepotism is a reminder that family plays a very important role to us.

It may seem like Hollywood is keeping current by including so many scenes of families at the dinner table, each one with their noses to a screen. In a way, the screenwriters are keeping things modern, but in another sense, this is yet another factor that normalizes the disturbing trend. It makes it seem okay; what isn't okay is the scourge of depression that invades so many households. How is it that we can feel so alone in a busy house? All you need to do is to ask the average teenager. I mean really have a meaningful conversation. It is difficult, primarily because we have almost completely forgotten how to connect to others.

Screens, yet again, play more than one role in making this a reality. One factor is our attention spans. How many times have you witnessed something in real life and just reached out for the rewind button only to find there is none? What about being part of a conversation, the first minute or two is easy, right? What about if they just go on and on; you tend to tune out, don't you? But, that is just because they are really boring, I get it. There are some people that just need to learn what to do to keep people interested. But, what if it isn't their job to entertain you? You might be in a lecture or classroom. Maybe you are attending on-the-job training? There is no getting away from needing to pay attention to people. The higher you climb on the corporate ladder the more you get paid to listen to people - sales or marketing meetings; board meetings; there are so many cases that strategic management requires you to pay attention to people that are not concerned about entertaining you.

How long do you concentrate for any significant period of time on anything other than a TV series, movie, or game? There is a lot of money involved in the entertainment industry - it can be said it is their job to keep your attention captivated. How well do you concentrate on work or studies? Constant notifications train us to drop one thing and move to another. We build habits of not completing tasks in one sitting. There is always a call coming in, or a friend texting, or a YouTube channel notification popping up. And those highly addictive game timers we covered earlier - the ones geared towards hijacking your 'achievement' mental system - even those ones are a pop-up notification by default.

Attention Deficit Disorder (ADD) is an abnormality of the previous generation; today, we are synthetically creating the mental habits, on a mass scale, that emulate the mental condition. It is quite self-evident that an inability to concentrate on others is the perfect way to avoid deep connections. Society began to operate on a very superficial level. What someone is wearing is more interesting than their ambitions in life, no? Think of when you go out with your friends, what are the topics you talk about? Crushes; cute guys/girls; fashion; stock trading advice; irritating people from work/school; political candidates?

When was the last time you had a deep conversation about something that brought a tear of joy or sorrow to your eye? When was the last time you felt emotionally moved by interacting with a family member? Do you ever remember being comfortable enough with someone to open yourself up to being truly vulnerable? You might be inclined to believe that there are people that need intimacy and those that don't. That is not the case.

If you turn on a reality show, what do you see? Superficial relations between friends and family, most likely, so this is normal, right? Normal, no; but common, yes. Do you know what else is common? Poor general mental health is common. Depression is common. Being unhappy is common. It is time to let go of what is 'common,' and to begin to analyze what progress has helped us and which of the social evolutions of the information age are ticking timebombs.

There is a fundamental element to strong mental health that comes from the role of the hormone oxytocin. This is a 'happy drug' that is produced by our brain that facilitates the feeling of being content and connected to others. The most common and natural stimulus to release this chemical comes from physical touch. It is the same hormone that allows for the bonding process between a new baby and its mother.

Anything from a simple handshake to a hug causes this chemical to cascade through our bloodstream. It comes from a skin-to-skin contact that we deem voluntary and pleasant. It is self-apparent that this fundamental mechanism of our human herd-animal biology is incapacitated by the migration to digital socialization. Therefore, it is clear that there is a limitation to the extent one is capable of feeling connected when stuck on a phone all day. This is a problem that leads to feeling lonely when, on a cognitive level, one believes that they are constantly connecting with others. Can you see how this situation (of being lonely, no matter how much effort one puts into reaching out to others) can lead to depression and later suicidal inclinations? This situation creates the false internal narrative that it is hopeless to try to find empathy and connection in others - perhaps you are just different - broken in some way. Suicide seems like a natural answer to end this internal suffering and aguish - the ever-rising suicide rates add empirical backing to phenomenon that so many feel.

It is important to realize that without the physical components of socialization, much like the grooming rituals performed by primates, we feel that something is missing. So many tribal cultures, from around the world, have frequent and ritualized acts of community that often involve physical interactions that form the very basis of their cultures. It is odd that the modern western world feels superior in its elimination of these 'superstitious' practices, without realizing that the coincidental effect of these rituals is to ensure that the members of the community feel integrated and accepted by the community itself. We have the science to prove our need for genuine, physical human interaction. Yet, for the most part, we choose to ignore it.

Think of the 'new' innovations introduced into maternal ward practices: it was not so long ago that it was desirable to have the newborn baby taken from the mother and housed in a communal nursery. After which point, the most 'socially advanced' families would have the child nursed by a wet nurse and then raised by a governess. The society that this method produced was cold and uncaring. It produced an unempathetic empire-building culture that sought to indenture or enslave anyone that was deemed different while extracting the most valuable resources from the land that was colonized.

We, as a global society, first fought back for liberation from the colonial powers (which were monarchies in almost every example - tying back into our tendency to seek family connection and community, even in such a dysfunctional set-up). After having achieved liberation for ourselves, we sought to institutionalize basic human rights for all. I feel that this change in trend is, in no small part, a direct result of the change in the child-raising approach.

In our new ward practices, mothers are encouraged to have as much skin-to-skin interaction with the child as possible, particularly within the first 24 hours. In very recent years, even the father is encouraged to bond in the same fashion. We are allowing our innate mechanism for developing empathy to flourish once again, after a disturbing period of modern history.

Research into the causes of bullying often tells a story of the perpetrator being a victim of their own set of circumstances. I would like to pose, to you, a hypothesis: bullying is an illustration of a twisted sense of empathy; a bully seeks company in their own suffering.

Our recent pandemic of COVID-19 aside, it has been put forward that we suffer a few pandemics of the modern era: obesity and cardiovascular disease; bullying; depression and suicide. How many of these seem to be linked to an unmentioned pandemic of screen addiction?

I hope I have made adequate links between poor physical health, albeit an improving trend with the introduction of such innovations as Fitbits, Wii Fit and Sweatcoins, and the like. I must admit, technology is playing a part in reducing the obesity problem.

A feeling of disconnection, and of having wasted one's time and effort on meaningless screen obsessions, leads to sadness and a feeling of depression that can manifest into suicidal tendencies. However, can you see how a hurt and sad person that feels all efforts towards the positive things in life are hopeless may also tend towards bullying others? If life is not fair, why should those 'lesser' than this suffering person have an easier and happier life?

Just like I cannot stress enough the harm that screen-addictions cause, I cannot over-stress the importance of building a healthy and proper physical community.

Unfortunately, it is easy to take an apathetic approach to a dysfunctional situation, all too often we believe that if we are alive without a proper connection with anyone else then we do not need it. This is simply a false string of logic that mirrors the reasoning of the short-sighted subconscious rationale.

It is saddening to see a family sitting around the dinner table all with a phone in hand. It is 'normal' now, a sign of modern progress. Just turn on any family sitcom and you will likely see scenes like that. Worst of all, the tone adopted is that of the parents being "wet blankets" and "old-fashioned" for requesting that the children put their screens away for an hour of the day. But the reality is that they don't, all too often the children learn the phones-at-the-table trend from their parents. There are many reasons, but are there any good reasons for texting or calling someone in the same house as you? After all, we are great at justifying anything that we want to do. There are very few, highly circumstantial, reasons that one would *actually* need to do so - and, even then, it would only be on an *ad hoc* basis.

Think of your family: how many hours a week are you dedicated to community/family time? This time does not need to be a productive time, in a traditional sense, it can be as simple as a chat about how everyone's day went. It can be a shared meal, where everyone helps with the preparation and clean-up. I would avoid activities such as movies or TV time, as this is quite distracting and impersonal - I am sure you can relate, right?

Family game nights are a fun way to experience other member's interests. This is my favorite option: everyone gets a chance to dictate the event's itinerary. We can endure anything for an hour or two. I would suggest a soft limit on things like Xbox; playing 'couch co-op' games with a hot seat set-up can bring families together. If you choose to allow this (I would limit it to once a month, given that it is screen-based), varying the conditions to hot-seat helps with inclusion - for example, first round the winner carries through; second round the loser plays the new challenger; then both round-two players tag-out for the third round. Change it up to avoid sibling rivalry taking over if one family member is destined to play every round under winner-plays-new-challenger rules. You can play games like Tekken or a racing game. If you have a Wii, there are many couch co-op options that allow for a bit of physical exercise too.

I have introduced this type of model to friends, it is fun to have family versus family events too. When introducing this, there are so many requests, especially from the children, that uncover common interests that the family never knew they shared. One of my favorite examples is the resurgence of Dungeon & Dragons, the Tabletop Game. One aspect is that parents tend to remember the trend as 'nerdy.' I personally love this game, or a home-brewed adaptation of it. The value of a role-playing game is to allow each individual to express creativity and build problem-solving skills.

I personally do not stick to the official rules, instead my family has a quick discussion as to how they want to play. The mechanics are adapted or invented in-game. The point is to create a shared world and to have far more freedom than any pre-coded game (this is one reason that the children of today enjoy such activities). You can even play a *My Little Pony* adaptation, these games can be made age-appropriate. It may take a few sessions to stumble through the rules you all collectively agree upon, but half of this process is discovering what each member values.

Personally, I advise that parents do some research into play therapy; I would advise not taking it too seriously though. For example, if your 13-year-old son describes a very brutal attack that his orc barbarian makes against a villainous dragon, it doesn't equate to a tendency towards walking into school on Monday to stab the teacher - this could just be an outlet for pent-up frustration, or (and this may be common) he could just be role-playing a movie or game that he has been exposed to. In this age of not being able to completely shelter children, unless you choose an off-the-grid and isolated lifestyle, it is important to help them properly digest the violence and other disturbing elements that they will come into contact with. When was the last time you took inventory of the socio-cultural context of a modern cartoon - the ones intended for toddlers? You may be shocked at the content.

So how do you integrate all of this into one fun activity? Try LARPing! LARPing stands for live-action role-playing, and this is a very fancy name given to the type of playtime that toddlers tend to trust on parents anyway: "Daddy, you are a pony. Be a pony!" These tend to get much more complex the older you go in age range, however. Some LARP groups double as camping getaways where you can do cosplay and enact fun adventures in fantasy settings.

You can try out arts and craft elements to make items, props, and costumes as a family. You then get to use them in your games. Some families may like pure imagination, sitting around a table - possibly going as far as using salt shakers, and the like, as markers - and others may want to head to the Halloween store early, or late, to pick up 'proper' props and costumes.

There are two aspects to role-playing as a family that really appeal to me. Firstly, it provides another healthier form of instantly gratifying the desire for achievement (as electronic games are so expertly designed to do). When the princess saves the prince from the mean dragon, your child gets the same thrill of having endured a journey to have their effort validated by achieving success. This makes this type of activity a decent substitute (in the mind of most teens and children) to the screen-based alternatives. The point is to adequately substitute the behaviors we are addicted to with activities that cater to the same reasons we chose those addictions in the first place.

The second is to provide a level of anonymity that acts like an insulating mask that lets us express interests and character aspects that may not be 'acceptable' in normal settings through the role-playing dynamic. A lawyer can choose to be a chaotic-neutral rogue in-game. And a person of small stature can assume a brutish build with super-human strength. While there are very solid rules governing these types of role-playing titles, I personally prefer coming to an agreement as to how this imaginary world will operate - when all is said and done, the idea is to have some fun.

While it may take a bit of effort to bring everyone to the table, more often than not it becomes an appointment the whole family enjoys keeping. You could also hand the mantle of "Games Master / Dungeon Master" (DM / GM - if you want to YouTube some tutorials) over to one of the kids. It will be a welcome change of the family dynamics, especially from their perspective. This also allows them to seek vengeance on any perceived heavy-handed parenting to which they may feel that they have been subjected, powerlessly. At the end of the day, you can probably put up with a GM that loves killing off your character whenever they can rather than trying to handle a 'terrible teen.' Or does winning the fantasy game mean more to you than an easier time governing the household? If it gets to the point that things get a bit over the top and no one is having any fun anymore, draw up a rotation schedule. Sure you all might suffer a TPK (total party kill) once every three or four sessions, but you can all just get used to playing mini-campaigns - think of Game of Thrones: it was entertaining even if all your favorite characters died just as soon as you grew to love them. Allowing your children a god-like ability to seek vengeance on any perceived injustices of the real world could prove a lot cheaper and more effective than any traditional therapy, it is just a game after all.

Other suggestions for game night would be learning card games, like poker, bridge, or canasta. It would surprise you how well a 10-year-old can play with a few month's practice. Games that rely on bluffing will help them to read non-verbal cues, which is an indescribably important skill for any career where they will need to deal with people - that is pretty much every career. If you can remember our section on the ease of miscommunication via text, you may see this as a fun way to build a strong sense of non-verbal communication.

Board games are also very successful choices; again, there are valuable skills to develop through these games. Monopoly is an age-old icon that is still relevant in teaching the basics of money-maintenance and strategic resource deployment. This is great for developing skills that a project manager or strategic-level manager would need to run a team. There is a good reason companies like Hasbro are still in business.

Trading card games might be a passion within the family - I would suggest adding to the collector's collection over birthdays and Christmas (or any occasion that you would normally give a gift). The present will likely be greatly appreciated, and with every addition, the collection will grow to accommodate more players - you might want to ask which add-ons or boosters they would like though, but that is up to you. The child (or adult...) would love to teach the family about their collection and running over in-game strategy and rules. Again, this puts the proverbial boot on the other foot as the child will experience a position of authority and expertise in a family dynamic that may not normally allow for such. Allow them to shine, this will help with confidence when dealing with others, especially those in authority (such as in executive presentations).

The simpler classics, like chess and checkers, that are traditionally a one-on-one set up can be hot-seated, or a knock-out pool progression can be used. You can draw lots to determine play-offs for each round or the kids can elect who plays whom. I don't need to point out that these types of strategy games are famous for teaching forward-planning.

As mentioned, TV-time is not the best choice, but it can be used on a winter's evening when the whole family snuggles up together for a movie or show everyone enjoys - I must stress this to be occasional. The idea is to replace screen-time, not to communalize it - it is a slippery slope when the addiction gets further accepted as a means to bring the family together. So just be cautious. The best would be to sync everyone's personal screen-time allocation and to do something together in the event of family screen-time.

It is also always best to socialize with friends whenever possible on a face-to-face basis. Social media and video-calling technology do wonders for keeping in touch with those too distant; it is by no means an adequate total substitute. As we have seen in the depression statistics over COVID-19 lockdowns, a person can only feel so connected using virtual means alone.

The major theme of this chapter is to advise substituting the screen-time that you are cutting out with activities that provide the same stimuli that drove you to the addiction in the first place, as well as to plan these activities to have a long-lasting positive effect on the future you. And above all, realize that, while it may seem so at times, you are not alone. There are people that care for you and you are capable of forming new relationships with true community as the goal. Pay attention to others and they will likely give you the attention that benefits you. Becoming vulnerable with the right sort of people will grow into building trust in your life. I may not know you personally, but know that

I wrote this book to help you become happier and more fulfilled.

Chapter 9:

Keeping a Routine

Earlier, you read that in the beginning phase, kicking an addiction relies heavily on routine. However, your work isn't done when you've broken free of the addiction. To avoid a relapse, you need to be planning consistently! Make planning itself a daily part of your routine and plan your days well in advance. Keeping a daily planner makes this process much easier, as you can check back with it and cross things off your list as you go.

It's a known fact that the most successful people on the planet keep a strict schedule, one that optimizes their time to the fullest. Successful people understand that time is their most precious resource, a truth you should be coming to realize now that you've spent a little more time being present with the world!

People recovering from addictions are at an exceptionally vulnerable point in their lives and must develop solid routines to avoid relapse. There must be no exceptions made to this plan. When you make one exception, you're more likely to allow for more and more - and this is how relapse happens. Especially with regards to smartphone addictions! Before you've had the time to fully enjoy your freedom, you'll have lost it again.

To avoid this, we'll go over several ways to structure your time effectively, as well as how to make planning a fulfilling exercise in itself so that you keep doing it! A great way to do this is by bullet journaling.

Basically, a bullet journal is a fully customizable booklet with grid dots on every page. Artistic people especially thrive on these little guys because of the crafty nature of going through every page and drawing out their own templates. The process of writing out one's schedule and filling up their journals has therapeutic qualities as well. For the person recovering from phone addiction, this may be the perfect distraction from the screen and outlet for your feelings.

If bullet journaling is too artsy for your tastes, you can always simply make yourself daily to-do lists during your evenings. This does the same thing as a bullet journal does for your day-to-day life. You can make your lists simple or even find templates for them either online or in stores. Whatever you choose to do, just make sure that it is a pleasurable experience for you, so that you make a habit of doing it.

Example Routine From Monday-Friday

6:00 am: Wake up!

6:00 am - 6:30 am: Hydrate and eat breakfast. No phone at all.

6:30 am - 7:30 am: Light exercise. No phones here, either.

7:30 am - 8:00 am: Shower. Brush your teeth. Get yourself prepared for the day. No phone!

8:00 am - 8:30 am: Respond to important work-related emails and phone calls if you have them. Log in to your student portals to check on assignments or due dates. You can only use your phone here for those purposes.

8:30 am - 9:00 am: Commute to work or school. If you don't need to commute, set yourself up for a productive day. No phones here!

9:00 am - 12:00 pm: Work or study. If you need to take a minute to break up the three hours, you should do so without a phone. Instead, use that time to hydrate and get a snack if you need it. Snacks help boost productivity!

12:00 pm - 12:30 pm: Take a lunch break. This is free time for you, so if you finish eating quickly you can use your phone to call or text your friends and family. Your phone is allowed here, but don't use social media. Using it now will tempt you through your day.

12:30 pm - 2:30 pm: Work or study some more. No phone! At the end of this, take a small fifteen-minute break for snacks and water.

2:45 pm - 5:00 pm: Work or study. When the clock hits five o'clock, make sure that you stop what you're doing. You've just had a very productive first day, so it's important that you give your mind a break to let it absorb all that information. No phones!

5:00 pm - 5:30 pm: Commute back home. If you work or study from home, use this time to disengage yourself by going for a small walk or listening to some music. No phone needed!

5:30 pm - 6:30 pm: Make a nice dinner. If you live with family or share food with roommates, make a routine of cooking your evening meals together. No phones, you don't need to burn yourself from the distraction!

6:30 pm - 10:00 pm: This is your time. Use it to spend time with your family or friends. If you work from home, try to get out of the house a little bit and get some fresh air. Organize your time for tomorrow with a to-do list or a journal. You can use your phone here, but only if you have nothing else to be present for.

10:00 pm - 11:00 pm: Use this time to shower again if you like, brush your teeth, and prepare to sleep. You might like to make yourself a tea or warm beverage to cozy up before you hit the hay. Don't use your phone here. Phones are proven to make sleep more difficult, so don't allow that to happen to you.

Example Routine from Saturday-Sunday

Assuming you don't also work on weekends, then these two days are completely free to you for your purposes. However, you should still make the effort to make a routine of them. Here's an example of a routine you can follow:

7:00 am: Wake up.

7:00 am - 8:00 am: Hydrate and make yourself a nice breakfast. Use this time to really pamper yourself. You've worked a hard week and you deserve a hearty breakfast! No phones here, especially while eating.

8:00 am - 9:00 am: Do your daily hygiene things but with a twist. Like with your meal, you should use this time to pamper yourself. Take a long and relaxing shower. Brush your teeth. Take some extra time for skincare. Everything that makes your body feel good, do it. No phone.

9:00 am - 12:00 pm: Do some things you love to do! For religious and faithful folks, get your spiritual needs in. Clean up your living space. Practice your hobbies and crafts. Maybe even take up new things, if you have the energy for it. Your phone is okay to use here, but again, keep your use of social media minimal.

12:00 pm - 5:00 pm: Hang out with your family or your friends! Make sure you meet with people to get some healthy and much-needed social time in. Have lunch. Go out to a cafe, or for a walk. Do all you can to be present with what you do. No phone here. When you spend time with others, you should make sure your phone is away to get the full value of the interaction.

5:00 pm - 6:30 pm: Make a big dinner. Ideally, you'll be doing this with the people you live with. Perhaps even invite a friend over! No phone here, either.

6:30 pm - 10:00 pm: More spare time for your family or for your hobbies. You can use your phone here! Relax from your day.

10:00 pm - 11:00 pm: Get ready to end your day. Make yourself a tea, relax with a book. Brush your teeth! Take a shower.

Weekends are obviously much more customizable than your Monday-Fridays. The urge to be on your phone will be much more tempting, so it's important to remain busy with things you love to do. You should try to keep your work to a minimum on weekends for the sake of conserving your energy, but there's nothing wrong with doing some homework and catching up on some emails if you have to.

Whatever you do, treat yourself. Reward yourself for your week by taking extra good care of yourself. Pamper yourself shamelessly with your hobbies and the time you spend with others.

The Spoon Theory Analogy

The schedule laid out is very in-depth, and it's certain not to meet everyone's needs. It is simply an example so that you can see how thoroughly a person recovering from smartphone addiction may need to allocate their time to make it through their day productively.

You may have noticed that there are several breaks mentioned throughout the day that include no phone. Your brain needs time between their work sprints to be able to absorb the information it has just received and to process it on an ongoing basis. It can only do this productively if you supply yourself with the nourishment and hydration that your body requires. It's not often thought of, but your brain needs a lot of energy! Keeping your body hydrated and nourished will help provide your brain with the energy it needs to keep doing its job all day, which essentially translates to how you feel throughout your workday. Purposeful breaks with the intent to refuel, so to speak, lend positively to your overall mood.

It's also important to feel like a human being while you're going through your day. It's tempting to go through a full day working long hours without breaks, especially during recovery. However, substituting one addiction for another is not the goal of this routine. If you allow yourself time throughout your workday to recharge, you'll feel less like a workhorse and you'll be more willing to continue working this way on a daily basis as a result.

Take note of your mental and physical needs as you're planning out your days. We all like to believe that we can be hyper-productive workaholics on a dime, but this isn't a healthy mindset to adopt. You're human, a living breathing creature. You have needs you must cater to!

Your needs are unique. After you've contemplated this schedule and you feel some of it falls short of your needs, then there's no shame in adjusting the schedule as you require. The important thing to keep in mind as you schedule is that you're not adjusting your schedule so that you can be on your phone more, as that's counter-productive. But, if you need to work up to a full eight-hour workday, then try cutting that time in half instead. Or breaking up your workday into two chunks. Use the rest of your time doing things that re-energize you, like a hobby that you love.

A great idea to keep in mind while recovering from any addiction is spoon theory, an analogy written by Christine Miserandino to describe life with chronic illness. In mental health, spoon theory is used to describe a person's energy levels and exertion throughout the day. Though this is primarily used for people who suffer from chronic illnesses, even people without tend to run out of energy as well. The theory is, therefore, applicable.

In this theory, the "spoon" categorizes one unit of energy. When you have your full set of spoons, you have enough energy to do all that you need to do in a day. When you're all out of spoons, you need to run the dishwasher, so to speak, by doing things that recharge you or by simply resting.

Spoon theory is wonderful because it teaches you to be more in-tune with your energy levels and your needs throughout the day. It also requires a degree of self-acceptance and self-care to acknowledge that maybe today you simply don't have the energy to do all the things on your to-do list, and you need to take more breaks or time to do other things. There's nothing wrong with this, nor adjusting your schedule accordingly.

No one was made into a super productive workforce overnight, and neither will you. It's unreasonable to expect perfection from yourself immediately. Even those who do not struggle with addiction can struggle with a perfect routine, especially when it comes to a healthy work-life balance.

You'll need to assess yourself on a daily basis to see what works and what doesn't work for you, and be brutally honest. If you acknowledge where you are on a constant basis, it makes it easier to know what your next steps are. For example, runners never start with running for a full three miles a day. They train up to it. Runners start as walkers, become light joggers after their stamina has increased, and then transition into running. Increase the time you can spend on doing your productive tasks like working or household chores by intervals that work for you. Maybe you do thirty more minutes every day. Maybe you do five. There's nothing wrong with this, as long as you're focusing on the growth.

Self-Help Groups and Therapy

Keep in mind that while recovering, the recovery process in of itself is draining of energy. It takes a lot of willpower to tell yourself not to do something - compulsive behaviors wouldn't be called 'compulsive' if they were easy to ignore, after all.

Another consideration is the incorporation of support groups into your week. There are groups that specialize in smartphone addiction recovery such as Camp Grounded, the Restart Center, and Morningside Recovery. These facilities tend to have a step program in much the same way that Alcoholics Anonymous and other addiction recovery programs do, but you may find that the true worth of these programs comes from the social interactions you'll have with other addicts.

You may also find something locally. Meet-ups and clubs are run in every town, so snoop around your area to see if there's any that you can join that are run specifically for people recovering from their smartphone addictions. This option is the cheaper option to joining a facility.

There are also therapists who specialize in cognitive behavioral therapy, the type of therapy which you will be doing to yourself while you alter your habits. This form of therapy has proven useful in treating hardcore addicts of smartphones and the internet. Consider speaking to your doctor for a referral to a therapist or shopping around for a therapist who specializes in dealing with addictions.

Something to keep in mind while considering your therapy options is that cognitive behavior therapy has several different types of approaches, and some may benefit you more than others. Cognitive behavior therapy has evolved to incorporate different techniques and methods of therapy outside of the clinical setting. Some examples of this are music and art therapy, and recreational approaches to therapy like exercise rehabilitation. If you're the type of person who needs something to do with their body and hands, these options may be perfect for you. You don't need to be skilled necessarily to partake in these therapies, either. Therapists that offer these options are willing to teach you what you need to know in order to start therapy in these different avenues - and if you end up falling in love with what you're doing in therapy, all the better! You've just found something you can spend time doing in your spare time that doesn't include a smartphone.

If you do choose to look for a therapist, keep in mind that therapists are people, too. Sometimes you won't find a therapist that jives well with you. That's to be expected in any setting where you work with another person, so don't be discouraged if one therapist isn't the right fit for you. Or if two aren't. Even if three aren't. Keep looking for a therapist that works well with you. Therapists are meant to work with you to help you find new behavior patterns that work well and keep you mentally healthy, so you should find someone that you like.

You may be tempted to join online groups for this purpose. This is counterintuitive, however. You'll be creating a dependency on screen time by using the internet for your therapeutic purposes, which contradicts the reason you sought therapy in the first place!

If there are no local options for groups and you can't afford therapy, ask a friend or a family member if they would be willing to support you by distracting you and being a confidant. Chances are, your friends are eager to support you and be there for you! Let them take you out to places, and take them out to places in return.

Focusing on spending time with others in real-time and learning how to become inspired during time lulls is the best way to keep yourself from falling back into the scrolling habits that come with smartphone addiction. While you're recuperating from addictive behaviors, find ways that you can fill your time creatively and socially. You're going to have to try several things before you find a routine that works for you, and there's nothing wrong with that. In fact, you should spend time figuring out for yourself what a good daily schedule looks like for you so that you can keep on that routine without introducing yet more stress in your life.

Allow yourself to embrace the process. There are certainly going to be ups and downs, but you can absolutely get over your smartphone and screen time addiction with some effort and self-patience.

Chapter 10:

The Aftermath

It's not over 'til the fat lady sings… I think that is an opera theater reference, but I am sure you catch my drift. The funny thing about the past is that it changes every day. Earlier, we covered the aftermath of your addiction and how it affected your life and those around you. Forgiveness is a key aspect to a successful and long-term recovery, especially the forgiveness of yourself. The great thing is that you have the chance, every day, to forge a new life and leave a new type of wake.

There is a truism that has captivated the creative minds of every media outlet, it's everywhere: "Today is the first day of the rest of your life."

There is also a paradox called: *The Pink Elephant Paradox.* If I asked you not to think of a pink elephant, one of two things would happen. One, you are completely perplexed by the absurdity of the request and, thus, did not picture a pink elephant or, anything at all, truly. Your mind is still reeling from trying to process the odd instruction. Or two, you did, in fact, picture the prohibited pink elephant. Either way, the words "pink elephant" were likely featured in your internal dialogue. Why is this?

It follows an interesting principle that boils down to your brain not being wired to process negatives. Any NLP or hypnosis practitioner worth their salt will tell you as much.

So, when those of your grandparents' generation rant-via-query: "Why are these young'uns always on their phones? Why don't they go outside and play?" they are not too far off the mark. It sounds ridiculous; and, no doubt, there has been plenty of ridicule that has followed this line. But, ridicule aside, there is a solid point here. If you were to spend the day internally chanting: "Don't go on my phone. Don't go on my phone. Don't..." Your efforts are fueling the fire of thinking about your phone. Which, in turn, fuels your desire to go on your phone.

The solution is simple, "go outside and play." Well, not exactly that, but focus on something else rather than focusing on what you don't want. Your phone has robbed you of time, attention and energy, up till now. Start making up for it.

Here is where we cover the process of rebuilding the life you want. If we skip this step you will either backslide back into your addiction or, you will find something else (equally as addictive) over which to obsess.

When we free up this void that will be left by restricting your screen-time to a healthy level, you will need something else to fill the gap. If you do not place something of importance to you in the gap you will likely find that it gets filled by more 'junk' stuff. And, you might as well be back on your phone again.

Here is one suggestion: education. Yes, burn me at the stake for being that guy, but first, hear me out. We are in an age that has seen the question of qualification versus experience mashed together from a standpoint of the average employer. Yes, even 'entry level' positions now request 2-5 years experience, plus a certificate/diploma/degree. The employer often doesn't get what they want: they settle for the best applicant. However, you want to be the person that does always get what you want - so be smart about it.

You may very well find yourself in an interview asking: "So, you want a certificate for packing shelves?" What may surprise you is the expectant grin you see smiling back at you with: "Do you have such a certificate? Corporate would love that!" He may be an idiot, but you are the one interviewing to pack his shelves, so...

It is ridiculous, but it is the new way of life. Think about the career you want. Now think of the next level for you. Entry-level, if you are in school. Or, your next jump or lateral movement, if you are an adult. Go onto a job seeker's website, or onto a platform like LinkedIn: what education does the potential employer require, or what education does someone doing that job have?

Ideally, you would want to have this research done by the time you enter secondary school. Instead of dropping the subjects you don't like, work backwards. What career do you want? What higher education do employers look for? What subjects and GPA is needed to, comfortably, get into that course? What subjects does Future-you want to crush in school now?

Which educational facility is surprisingly irrelevant, so you can go to whatever college just to be with your 'boo.' But, make sure you get into the right course.

Okay, you might just want to be a billionaire without a qualification. That's fine. Some of the wealthiest and most influential people in the world don't have degrees. Step one: get into M.I.T. Step two: drop-out (but you have to get in first). After all, no other university in the world has such a prestigious reputation of breeding successful drop-outs (they must be doing something right if you don't even need to finish).

We live in a culture that states that we should do what we are good at, and we ought to love it too. The fact is, it's wrong. And, I don't say so lightly. Just because you have an aptitude for something does not mean that it will bring you any joy.

There is a premise that if you were to dedicate 10,000 hours to properly practicing any activity that you will achieve the capability of "world-class." Not to say that you will be the best in the world, but that you will be capable of achieving the standard required of an international competitor. Aptitude will simply shave a couple of hundred hours off this requirement. Think of it as a springboard, it gives you an extra boost. It does not dictate your life's direction. So if you need to bump up your math grade by a symbol or three, all it takes is effort using the correct tools and mentors.

You would be surprised at the learning and physical disabilities that some world-renowned icons have conquered. Writers and mathematicians with dyslexia, athletes, and musicians that had to miss seemingly vital limbs. Psychologists and philanthropists with personality disorders. For your YouTube allocation, I recommend searching a few; they are a wee bit more inspirational than funny cat videos. Think of these 'disabilities' as 'counter-aptitudes,' they merely add a few extra hours onto the amount needed to master anything you have the means to practice. You don't even need to practice in an orthodox fashion. If you are dyslexic and struggle with numbers you just need to find an unconventional method of tackling that problem - you can still achieve the scores you need.

The internet has given us access to the experiences and knowledge from people that were unfathomable a few decades ago, maybe the method you need to conquer your 'counter-aptitude' is exclusively available in Romanian - hooray for Google Translate! With enough determination and persistence, you can do anything; these are the only currencies that truly matter in the game of life.

Doing what makes you feel good about being yourself is what you need to aim for in order to lead a fulfilled and happy life. With enough practice, you can become good at anything, and once you become good at what you love you will be happy doing what you are (now) good at. Whether you believe in reincarnation, the afterlife, or are an atheist, there is one thing we can agree upon: you only get one go at today. This also applies to the rest of this lifetime. Dedicating yourself to a purpose that is close to your heart and that allows you to look in the mirror with pride will allow you to look back on your days without regret. What more could you ask for when leaving this world?

While smart devices teach us about the joys of instant gratification, would you agree they are great at teaching us about regret when we look back on all the days we squander doing nothing useful?

Perhaps you are not too concerned about a career, ambition is not in everyone's blood. Passion is, however. If you don't think so, it is just because you have not found your muse, yet. Let's fix that. What concerns you when you think of the world? Perhaps your vocation is already staring you in the face. Are you convicted in your faith? Religion and/or spirituality can provide you with a merry lifetime worth of work. You don't have to be a religious leader, if the prospect is not appealing, you could dedicate yourself to a quiet life of study or to a supporting role that facilitates a cause that is meaningful to you.

Perhaps you are more an appreciator of the arts, do you engage in any artforms? Does curating a museum or art gallery appeal to you? Maybe, you fancy yourself a healer by way of improving the lives of the less fortunate. Volunteering at the local soup kitchen or animal shelter is not the worst thing to do with your time, far from it actually.

This is the point where we start planning the future. I suggest choosing just one new goal, at first. Slow but steady is the way to go. It can be as simple as spending some real face-to-face time with friends or family.

Once you have a goal in mind, unless it is fairly straightforward and immediately actionable, use the SMART format for defining your goal. The SMART method is a term used to describe goal setting that is realistically achievable, time-sensitive, and acts as a step towards a large overarching dream. You can break it down into smaller objectives if you need.

The better the definition of what you want for your new and improved life, the better the chance that you will achieve it. Adding time expectations will make you more accountable, and being specific will give you clear criteria of whether you hit the mark or not.

The trick is to choose something that you are passionate about. The goal of getting into Yale (because your parents want you to go there) is not likely to inspire you to put in the persistent hard work needed to improve mediocre grades to the standard of being accepted into a top university. If every bone in your body oozes with the desire to get into Yale - you will probably already be well on your way of getting in - by hook or by crook. When you are looking into goals that you feel you might like to achieve, ask yourself why.

Why is this particular achievement important to you? Is it fame or fortune? Do you have a standard set that you feel you need to live up to; if so, whose? If it is your own standard that's great, if it is someone else's you need to do some more digging. Once you get to the bottom of why another person's standard is important to you, you will uncover your why. Is the opinion of your parents or friends important enough to drive you through to reach your goal?

There are a couple of reasons that an internal locus of control (being motivated by your own standards) is more beneficial than external loci of control (the external standards). It is impossible to escape every external locus - if you work within a system there is an external standard that has been set. If you decide to make your own rules by becoming an entrepreneur, you escape one level of external standards but you still need to provide a product or service that is wanted by the market. There will be a customer satisfaction aspect to consider in the equation of how well your company does.

Is it possible to become entirely internally motivated? Yes. It is as simple as adopting the external standards and making them your own. For example: if your parents are hell-bent on you going to a certain university (and you are interested in keeping them happy) then all you need to do is find your own 'why' behind achieving their plans for you. They might love the sports program. On doing some research you may find that their cultural program is just right for you, or that the location works for you. Do you like nature reserves?

The reason behind identifying your big 'why' is to get you up in the morning and to keep you off your screen. If you have a greater motivation driving your life, you will be able to do 3 hours of research on Google without feeling tempted to spend hours more being distracted and entertained by a screen.

When analyzing the life and achievements of any renowned individual from history books, or modern-day examples, it is easy to see some credence to the cynical assumption that these dedicated individuals are simply addicted to success; religious perfection; meditation; their own pipe-dream version of how the world ought to be; or whatever it may be.

As we have stated, the human body is wired for obsessive and compulsive behaviors. It is geared towards perpetuating behaviors that kept us alive yesterday under the assumption it will lead to being alive tomorrow. That is the only standard of success for our habit-forming program: stay alive. This program can lead to addiction, especially when other additional factors, like hormones, come into play.

That said, we can fine-tune this basic survival function into a tenacious driving force that boosts us out of bed every morning and gives us the push we need to overcome all the odds that are stacked against one person changing the world. Take Thomas Edison for example, after a thousand attempts it can be easily said that he may have been addicted to the idea of inventing a functioning lightbulb. Alexander the Great could be said to have been addicted to ruling the world; he was still able to take a small mountainous country and turn it into one of the largest, multicultural empires the world has ever seen, as short-lived as it was. These men were able to leverage their innate and indomitable 'addiction' into doing remarkable things.

You don't need to want to change the world, all you need is to really want to change yours in order to feel accomplished and fulfilled. It is unhappiness and a feeling of lack that lure us into unhealthy addictions; feeling good about who you are and what you do every day is key to avoiding slipping into bad addictions. We have spent the first few chapters covering the push factors that ought to drive you away from a tech addiction; it is up to you to find your own pull factor that draws you towards something meaningful and fulfilling.

Conclusion

By this point, it should be clear that allowing a screen-habit to develop is inviting a *bona fide* addiction into one's life. It creates a physical reliance and escalating resistance (through dopamine in particular) just like any hardcore addiction. A screen addiction also creates a mental dependence through our human habit-forming tendencies. Unlike most other addictions, a reliance on devices is very socially acceptable - it is very difficult to spot an addict versus a highly productive modern individual that harnesses the multitude of advantages that technology can provide. When in doubt, which is often, people tend to view addicts as eager tech-savvy modernists; this means that many addicts are unaware of the far-reaching problems that begin to take root until it is too late. This also means that this variety of addiction is not offered the same help that we all need when in the grasp of addiction.

As illustrated, this addiction has an almost unique danger of opening up a user to the criminal underworld. While buying illegal narcotics does the same, the internet has far more varieties of dangerous people prowling about for a victim. Unlike crossing over to the 'wrong side of the tracks' in order to get your fix, where added vigilance is instinctive, the online world offers predators the opportunity to approach even the most innocent within the confines and comfort of their own home. These criminals are offered an opportunity to disguise themselves as seen nowhere else: three-gnomes-in-a-coat is easy enough to spot in the real world, but it is very hard to discover exactly who is behind a profile. This is only exacerbated by the fact that individuals that have had their identity stolen and become aware of the fact are drawn to do something like upload a TikTok rant about how they are the real Joe Soap and they are aware of digital imposters. Unfortunately, as can be seen on selected episodes of MTV's *Catfish* these 'verification videos' can then be used by an imposter that has been stalking their 'masks' real digital footprints. It is scary how 'real' a fake profile can seem.

If predators and human traffickers were not a big enough threat, there is the dark web that houses anything from illegal pharmaceuticals and actual narcotics to murders-for-hire.

The fact is this: law enforcement has an uphill battle trying to stay in the game when it comes to combating online threats. They barely scratch the surface, even with all of today's advancements in cybersecurity. It is my most sincere hope that they are able to exponentially scale up their effectiveness soon. But, for now, we must face the reality that the internet is much like the lawless Wild West, way back when. It is a new frontier, after all.

To add fuel to the fire, there is a strong double-mindedness from any major corporation that provides the digital infrastructure and hardware to which we can become addicted. One side of the equation is the sales aspect: Big-Tech has the interests of its stakeholders and its own aims of monopolization to consider. The reason companies like Facebook, Apple, and Microsoft still exist is because they are profitable. Ever-growing cyclic consumption is the name of the game - they need to move physical products and provide a substantial audience for their ad investors. On the other hand, they do have a responsibility to society to self-regulate the adverse effect of their business models. There are even some White House examples illustrating that there are always casualties when large amounts of money collide with social responsibility and ethics.

I am sure you can think of plenty of examples of the dynamics I have just mentioned, but there is a very powerful undercurrent that keeps the criminal section of the dark web alive and well. Namely, currency - more particularly the favored currency of the illegal trade online: cryptocurrency. You may, or may not, be aware that the FBI and Interpol have a much harder time tracing cryptocurrency than they do *forex* (Dollars, Euro, Pounds, etc.). It is a myth that crypto (like Bitcoin) is completely untraceable, but it does sidestep a lot of anti-money-laundering protocols that have slowly developed as the information age evolved.

When you think of the major pressure that key investors put onto institutions like the government and Wall Street to legitimize cryptocurrency (to the same level as traditional currency, like the USD), it hints at the fact that these companies may not be interested in preventing the use of their commodity to such a large trading market. Logically, a company would not want to ban their most fanatic consumers only to fight viciously to be recognized in a market that is far more skeptical.

I am not pointing any fingers, after all, bales of dollar bills are seized in cocaine busts every year, but it is a disturbing fact that a lot of the demand for cryptocurrency comes from ne'er-do-wellers. Until such time when cryptocurrencies are firmly recognized in the more legitimate marketplaces, crypto-companies may find research into preventing criminal activity on the back burner. Truth be told, I think that if they did successfully remove their product from the criminal underground it would result in such a drastic reduction in the perceived value of crypto that the entire industry could implode. For example: if for every one bitcoin used on a legitimate market two are used on the criminal market one may find that two-thirds of the bitcoin dried up overnight. With such a drastic drop almost everyone would dump their stock and the commodity would become worthless. This is purely hypothetical, no one really knows how much money (of any kind) is used on the black market, but suffice to say, you can see why the *Dark Web* is not going anywhere anytime soon.

Briefly, we have recapped a few factors behind tech addiction. The point I want to make with all of this is: no one else is interested in taking care of you (or your children); they have too many focuses of their own, whoever they are. Not even law enforcement has the ability, at present, to mitigate the risk down to anything we are used to in the physical world. No patrol cars are surfing the WiFi waves. It falls to us, you and me, as responsible and concerned citizens to protect ourselves and those we love from the dangers of the new tech revolution.

You may have heard the statement that the technology in our cell phones outstrips the capacity of what was used to land a man on the moon - it might startle you to realize that that statement was from the 'brick' age. No touchscreens. Back then, it was conceivable that there may have only been one or two cellular phones per household. Now, we need a SmartWatch to connect to our SmartPhone so that our SmartTV can tell us how many steps we took to get from the kitchen to the living room - one or two devices per individual is common, possibly even lacking, in this age. It shocked me to see the long list of connected devices when I reviewed my Google account, that was one of the first indicators that I was becoming an addict. Try it, see if you remember how many devices you have. With sales targets shooting through the roof, you can bet that technology companies are doing everything they can to give you as many opportunities to become addicted. An addict (with money) is good for business.

I have given you the three major techniques for combating this ever-growing temptation. Firstly, we have our #BrickChallenge, this method is the good-old cold-turkey approach. You just stop, let the withdrawal kick in, and ride it through. Once you are done, your dopamine receptors should be more sensitive again, and so the physical temptation is lessened. If you carry this challenge through to six weeks, your neural network in your brain that had been wired for this connection will be reconfigured, and so your mental temptation is lessened.

Our second method was substitution; I had given you a schedule detailing allowable screen times and non-screen times. Following this method is a softer approach to the first and it works in the same way. You will only reap the rewards in a more gradual manner due to only gradually limiting screen-time, but it is easier to stick to for those not cut out for cold-turkey. A good plan that you follow is better than the perfect plan you don't.

Lastly, we covered the transcendence method. It is probably the oldest of them all, predating the definition of 'addiction' by my estimate, but there is a very good reason it is still around. Addiction operates in the realms of physical urge and mental pseudo-logic. Your body wants it and your mind gives you all the reasons you need not to say "no." Using this mindfulness approach we get the same physical and neurological benefits from the cold-turkey approach. As a bonus, we can avoid a lot of the 'struggling' that is involved with "fighting" the addiction; plus, we build up our willpower muscle. We simply use the will-over-mind-over-body model and allow the thoughts about doing anything against our will to pass down the river. The trick is to not get attached. Don't grapple or fight, just let it flow past you while staying resigned to the *Nike* slogan: "Just do it." You made a decision concerning what you want from life and have identified what you must do (and what you must avoid) in order to get it - just stick with your decision.

There is no one perfect method. Yes, some people swear by any one of these, but the fact is we are all unique. One of these will work for you - it will take hard work, but if you work the method, it will work for you. Which one? I can't say. They all might work, or perhaps only one will; we are different and that is why I have given you options. If for some reason, none of them work, it is probably because you are not addicted - you know you just spend too much time on your phone. You know you should stop it, so stop it. There we go, all possibilities are covered!

But, seriously, I cannot express how grateful I am that you have joined me on this journey. As a concerned citizen, I am proud that you have chosen to help change the trajectory that we have been following before it is too late. We can rediscover human intimacy and connection within a technologically advanced world by restricting one addiction at a time. Today is your day, all you have to do is be the best you, and even that is just for today. Tomorrow is just a new today, don't worry about it, it will be here in the morning - then you can tackle it as a new individual, made stronger by your decisions today.

Thank You

We at *A Concerned Citizen Publishing* are genuinely interested in how this system worked for you or for your children. We designed this program with all intentions in mind of ridding the world of unproductive human beings. It is truly sad to see an entire generation of kids and teens completely consumed by their devices. You can barely have a conversation with someone these days without them looking down at their phone every 30 seconds. I miss the old way of doing things and the old way of communicating on a day to day basis. It is our mission to get this way of life back, and to create a new beginning for all these addicted kids and teens. If you are passionate about this topic and happen to feel the same way after reading this book, take a minute to leave a kind review on Amazon. **https://www.Amazon.com/review/create -review/asin=**

It will help spread the word to others and hopefully save more lives in the process. We would love to hear your story and how this book resonated with you. Please feel free to contact us with your comments and opinions regarding this topic. We will keep you up to date with all of our success stories, and hopefully this will provide motivation for you and others to keep up the good work. Thanks again for being a part of this new movement, and creating a better life for yourself!

Feel free to come over and see us at concernedcitizenbooks.com . Sign up for the Fan Club to get discounts, free shipping, and monthly updates regarding new book releases / release dates. Thanks again, hope to see you soon!

References

Archer, D. (2013). *Smartphone Addiction.* Psychology Today.
https://www.psychologytoday.com/ca/blog/reading-between-the-headlines/201307/smartphone-addiction

Burns, B., Copeland, D., Fabelo, D., Hames, B., & Hullum, M. (Director). (2016). *Connected.* [Film]. RoosterTeeth.

E.H Danner Museum of Telephony. (n.d.). *Communication Before Telephones.* Angelo State University.
https://www.angelo.edu/community/west-texas-collection/museum-of-telephony/communication-before-telephones.php

Gaille, L. (2018). *19 Advantages and Disadvantages of Cell Phones.* Ittana.org Personal Finance Blog.
https://vittana.org/19-advantages-and-disadvantages-of-cell-phones

Kim, H. (2013). *Exercise rehabilitation for smartphone addiction.* Journal of Exercise Rehabilitation, *9*(6), 500-505. Department of Social Welfare,

Cheongam College. DOI: https://doi.org/10.12965/jer.130080

Kress, G. (2004). *Reading Images: Multimodality, Representation and New Media.* Information Design Journal, *12*(2), 110-119. DOI: https://doi.org/10.1075/idjdd.12.2.03kre

Martin, G., & Pear, J. (1978). *Behavior Modification: What It Is and How To Do It.* Routledge.

Miserandino, C. (n.d.). *The Spoon Theory.* ButYouDon'tLookSick.com. https://butyoudontlooksick.com/articles/written-by-christine/the-spoon-theory

Pensworth, L. (2020). *Guide to Smartphone Addiction: Statistics, Symptoms and Solutions.* DailyWireless. https://dailywireless.org/mobile/smartphone-addiction/

Postman, N. (1992). *Technopoly: The Surrender of Culture to Technology.* New York: Vintage Books.

Przepiorka, A., Blachnio, A., Miziak, B., & Czuczwar, S. (2014). *Clinical approaches to treatment of Internet Addiction.* Pharmacological Reports, *66*(2), 187-191.

Scudamore, B. (2018). *The Truth About Smartphone Addiction, And How To Beat It.* Forbes. https://www.forbes.com/sites/brianscudamore/2018/10/30/the-truth-about-smartphone-

addiction-and-how-to-beat-
it/?sh=2f2178814232

Young, K. (2007). *Cognitive Behavior Therapy with Internet Addicts: Treatment outcomes and Implications.* CyberPsychology & Behaviours, *10*(5), 671-679. doi:10.1089/cpb.2007.9971

Printed in Germany
by Amazon Distribution
GmbH, Leipzig